The Index Trading Course Workbook

Founded in 1807, John Wiley & Sons is the oldest independent publishing company in the United States. With offices in North America, Europe, Australia, and Asia, Wiley is globally committed to developing and marketing print and electronic products and services for our customers' professional and personal knowledge and understanding.

The Wiley Trading series features books by traders who have survived the market's ever changing temperament and have prospered—some by reinventing systems, others by getting back to basics. Whether a novice trader, professional, or somewhere in-between, these books will provide the advice and strategies needed to prosper today and well into the future.

For a list of available titles, visit our web site at www.WileyFinance.com.

The Index Trading Course Workbook

*Step-by-Step Exercises and
Tests to Help You Master*
The Index Trading Course

GEORGE A. FONTANILLS

TOM GENTILE

WILEY

John Wiley & Sons, Inc.

For general information on our other products and services or for technical support, please contact our Customer Care Department within the United States at (800) 762-2974, outside the United States at (317) 572-3993 or fax (317) 572-4002.

Wiley also publishes its books in a variety of electronic formats. Some content that appears in print may not be available in electronic books. For more information about Wiley products, visit our web site at www.wiley.com.

ISBN-13 978-0-471-74598-3
ISBN-10 0-471-74598-7

Printed in the United States of America.

10 9 8 7 6 5 4 3 2 1

To Ruth Cawood
who inspires us all to live up to our full potential.

Contents

Introduction

The Index Trading Course Workbook is designed to supplement its companion manual by offering concise summaries and practical exercises to help put your new knowledge into action. The "Media Assignments" are particularly useful in this regard. Be sure to run through each chapter in this workbook as you complete *The Index Trading Course* in order to reinforce the material.

There are two major reasons why you should increase your index knowledge. First, these market barometers are an important means for understanding big-picture trends along with more subtle market action. And second, it's simply about trading. Index-based products provide traders with an opportunity to capitalize on broad market and sector moves, leaving behind individual company risk. While there are no guarantees that a whole group of related companies won't be investigated by the SEC for bad accounting practices, we feel the chance of that is substantially lower than for a single company. Sector investing is where fundamental, technical, and sentiment analysis can really excel.

The Index Trading Course begins with a little index history à la Charles Dow, and then transitions to widely followed indexes in today's markets. Along the way, we investigate index construction, market trends, and general industry group coverage. The workbook reinforces your knowledge of core stock market indexes along with the sector offerings from a variety of financial entities. You also have the opportunity to incorporate foundational technical techniques into your analysis. Regardless of the complexity of indicators you use down the road, you can never move too far away from the basics.

The Index Trading Course quickly moves toward trading applications with coverage of index-based products, including exchange-traded funds (ETFs), index options, and ETF options. These different securities are used throughout the remainder of the text with appropriate trading strategies. Optionetics' low-risk, high-reward philosophy permeates the strategy discussions. The workbook serves to give the reader a working knowledge of these products, with tips and market characteristics (i.e., liquidity, percent weightings) provided by experienced traders.

Product detail and strategy information are the main focus of the middle portion of the text. Since *The Options Course*, *The Stock Market Course*, and *The Volatility Course* precede this book, we quickly run through option basics and move toward more advanced topics so more time can be spent on strategies, including the appropriate conditions for their use. It is suggested that traders new to options read these texts before incorporating such tools into their trading. Options are distinct from equities and have unique risks and characteristics that must be understood by the trader. This is true of any security or investment; traders must make it their responsibility to understand how a product or strategy works if they wish to be successful.

Exchange-traded funds are offered by a variety of groups, including exchanges, investment companies, and market data providers. Since the number of individual products is very large and growing, you should begin your focus with a family of ETFs that fit your style and branch out from that point. The focus for ETFs is primarily passive index tracking; however, as more products enter the marketplace, those who seek to beat a particular sector or style will likely grow more active. The workbook reinforces concepts of active and passive investing, along with a couple of strategies aimed at beating indexes in various sections.

At Optionetics, we are equal opportunity strategists. We will employ fundamental, technical, or sentiment analysis in our goal of trading profitability. We will even mix it up a bit—we don't care, we just want to protect our downside when the day is done. Profitable opportunities will follow.

All traders will find applications that suit their style in the workbook; some may be familiar and some may be new. Ideally, you will find that each analytical discipline has a place in your various market and trading assessments. In the "Getting an Edge with Indicators" section the reader is presented with a variety of techniques for gauging market strength, including newly developed tools that are readily available to investors with access to the Internet. So as not to leave nonsurfers out, our "Media Assignments" also seek to include those with more limited web access. *The Index Trading Course* also outlines system trading and system development to help analysts put their strategies to the test.

As *The Index Trading Course* and the accompanying workbook draw near to the end, "Making Adjustments," "Getting Started," and a few more lone index strategies are included to wrap things up. Chapter 16, "Getting

Started," provides information to new traders while also reminding the more experienced about paper trading resources. The workbook takes readers through the process of initiating a paper trade to get the habit established early and often. And true to form, we also include a "Risk Management" chapter (Chapter 14) complete with workbook exercises to test your skills in this area.

We hope that both *The Index Trading Course* and the accompanying workbook will be long-time references in your trading library. We're pretty sure indexes are here to stay. Happy trading!

The Index Trading Course Workbook

CHAPTER 1

A Look Back

SUMMARY

Over the years the stock market has evolved quite a bit—both structurally and in terms of the accessibility of information available to individuals. The Internet has further revolutionized the markets by providing instant access to news, data, and charts. In addition, the proliferation of indexes not only enables investors to gauge the health of their local markets, but also lets them easily monitor foreign markets as well. Even the instruments employed by individuals to invest and trade have evolved.

In this chapter, we take a brief look at the history of U.S. stock market indexes and explore the big picture of major current-day indexes. We also review information about the Dow Jones Industrial Average, the Dow Jones Transports, the NASDAQ Composite Index, and the S&P 500 Index. The concept of sectors and industry groups is introduced. A breakdown for one sector is provided. All of these market barometers—major indexes, sectors, and industry groups—are discussed throughout the book in greater detail. More importantly, these key topics are covered with the trader in mind.

THE INDEX TRADING COURSE WORKBOOK

QUESTIONS AND EXERCISES

1. Charles Dow developed the first index in 1884, which focused on
   _____ companies.
   A. Industrial.
   B. Railroad.
   C. Utility.
   D. All of the above.

2. Today, the Dow Jones Industrial Average consists of _____
   stocks.
   A. 500.
   B. 100.
   C. 30.
   D. 25.

3. Which of the following company stocks are included in the Dow
   Jones Industrial Average?
   A. Dow Jones & Company (DJ), Dow Chemical (DOW), and Jones
       Apparel Group (JNY).
   B. Pfizer (PFE), Verizon (VZ), and American International Group
       (AIG).
   C. Industrials, transports, and utilities.
   D. Apple Computers (APPL), Amazon.com (AMZN), and Microsoft
       (MSFT).

4. Match the index with its characteristics by drawing a line to the appropriate answer:
   A. Dow Jones Transportation   1. All stocks trading on one
       Average   specific market.
   B. Dow Jones Industrial Average 2. U.S. stock benchmark for pro-
   C. NASDAQ Composite Index   fessionals.
   D. S&P 500 Index   3. Evolved from the first index.
                                    4. 30 blue-chip stocks.

5. The use of a modified _____ adjusts the construction of the Dow Jones Industrial Average from a simple average to one that incorporates changes due to stock dividends and splits.

   A. Divisor.
   B. Index.
   C. Depreciation.
   D. Duration.

6. Dow theory postulates that movements in the Dow Industrials be confirmed by movements in the Dow Transports to validate a(n) _____ bull or bear market.

   A. Big.
   B. Bad.
   C. Ugly.
   D. Sustainable.

7. True or false: The Dow Jones Industrials cannot rise if the Dow Jones Transports fall.

8. The most comprehensive barometer of the health of the NASDAQ Stock Market is the _____ Index, which is often associated with the United States' leading technology companies.

   A. Dow Technology.
   B. NASDAQ Hi-Tech.
   C. NASDAQ Composite.
   D. OTC.

9. True or false: The S&P 500 Index is the underlying index for some of the most actively traded futures and options contracts in the world.

10. The S&P 500 Index is important to investors and professional money managers because it includes 500 _____.

    A. Mutual funds that track it.
    B. Of the largest companies trading on U.S. stock exchanges.
    C. Top NASDAQ companies within it.
    D. Popular sectors.

11. True or false: A sector is part of an industry group.

12. The technology sector includes _____ industry groups.
    A. Investment services, asset managers, and brokers.
    B. Fast-growth, low-risk.
    C. Software services, software, and computer hardware.
    D. Mature, low-risk.

13. True or false: The Dow Jones Industrial Average, the NASDAQ Composite Index, and the S&P 500 are all important market barometers for investors and traders and are worth monitoring.

14. Higher-priced stocks have a _____ weighting within the Dow Jones Industrial Average.
    A. Greater.
    B. Lesser.
    C. Insignificant.
    D. Biased.

MEDIA ASSIGNMENT

Media assignments are intended to help you put the material you've read into action by prompting you to access some of the extensive media tools available to you. These include financial papers, magazines, the Internet, and television. The tool with the most extensive information on any given day is the Internet. As the cost of a personal computer has fallen, the speed and power of home systems have increased. Access to the Internet has also improved and once you get online, a wide variety of financial-based web sites await you. There is no question that Internet access and a few key subscriptions greatly facilitate the process of researching and implementing trading ideas. We will, however, look at all forms of media when completing the exercises in the "Media Assignment" section.

The first media assignment requires a computer with an Internet connection and a printer, if available. As the primary task, you will be accessing four major Dow Jones averages and determining if there are any companies that appear on more than one of them. Once your PC is ready to go and you have online access, perform the following steps:

1. Type www.dowjones.com into the web browser. This will take you to the Dow Jones & Company, Inc. web site.

2. From the home page, click on the tab labeled "The Company" in the yellow strip.

3. Then click on the text "History/Timeline" that appears along the left side below the company's mission statement if you'd like to spend a little time reviewing this history.

4. Go to the text that coincides with 1884 and click on "Dow Jones Averages." This will launch a new browser on your screen. From here you can access historical Dow data, current levels for the major Dow Jones indexes, component information, and additional history about the averages.

5. Scroll down to the Investable Indexes Table and determine whether, on a daily basis and on a year-to-date (YTD) basis, there are any divergences among these first four averages.

6. Go to the last column on the tables—"More Info"—and determine how many components are in each index. Are there any components that appear on the Industrial Average, the Transportation Average, and the Utility Average? You many want to print out the component list for each to make this portion of the exercise easier. Are there any companies in any of these three indexes that also appear on the fourth index, the Dow Jones Composite Average? What conclusion can you make about the Composite Average?

VOCABULARY LIST

Average	Index
Blue chip	Industry
Dividend	Price-weighted
Divisor	Sector
Dow Jones Industrial Average	Stock split
Dow Jones Transportation Average	Ticker symbol
Dow theory	

SOLUTIONS

1. Charles Dow developed the first index in 1884, which focused on _____ companies.

   Answer: B—Railroad.

   Discussion: Charles Dow focused on the most important industry of the day—railroad companies—when he created his first index. This allowed him to simplify the process of reviewing the performance of all of the stocks in this group. The Dow Jones Industrial Average was the second index that Charles Dow constructed.

2. Today, the Dow Jones Industrial Average consists of _____ stocks.

   Answer: C—30.

   Discussion: The current-day Dow Jones Industrial Average (INDU) includes 30 large companies dominant in their fields. It includes stocks from both the New York Stock Exchange and the NASDAQ Stock Market. The NASDAQ Composite (COMPQ) includes all of the stocks on the NASDAQ Stock Market. The S&P 500 (SPX) consists of 500 stocks while the NASDAQ 100 consists of 100.

3. Which of the following company stocks are included in the Dow Jones Industrial Average?

   Answer: B—Pfizer (PFE), Verizon (VZ), and American International Group (AIG).

   Discussion: As of November 2005, these three companies are the latest additions to the Dow, replacing Eastman Kodak (EK), AT&T (T), and International Paper (IP). Financial, technology, pharmaceutical, and manufacturing companies are among groups represented in the present-day index. In January 2006, the complete list of companies was as follows: 3M Co.; Alcoa Inc.; Altria Group Inc.; American Express Co.; American International Group Inc.; AT&T Inc.; Boeing Co.; Caterpillar Inc.; Citigroup Inc.; Coca-Cola Co.; DuPont de Nemours & Co.; Exxon Mobil Corp.; General Electric Co.; General Motors Corp.; Hewlett-Packard Co.; Home Depot Inc.; Honeywell International Inc.; Intel Corp.; International Business Machines Corp.; Johnson & Johnson; JP Morgan Chase & Co.; McDonald's Corp.; Merck & Co. Inc.; Microsoft Corp.; Pfizer Inc.; Procter &

Gamble Co.; United Technologies Corp.; Verizon Communications Inc.; Wal-Mart Stores Inc.; and Walt Disney Co. This list will change over time.

4. Match the index with its characteristics by drawing a line to the appropriate answer.

    Answer: Connect each index as follows:

    A. Dow Jones Transportation Average—3. Evolved from the first index.

    B. Dow Jones Industrial Average—4. 30 blue-chip stocks.

    C. NASDAQ Composite Index—1. All stocks trading on one specific market (NASDAQ Market).

    D. S&P 500 Index—2. U.S. stock benchmark for professionals.

5. The use of a modified _____ adjusts the construction of the Dow Jones Industrial Average from a simple average to one that incorporates changes due to stock dividends and splits.

    Answer: A—Divisor.

    Discussion: A modified divisor helps to ensure continuity in the average after mergers, stock splits, and dividends. Rather than summing the number of companies in this index, the calculation uses a specific divisor value that is updated when any of its component stocks undergoes a corporate action (i.e., dividend, split, etc.). In this way, the Dow Jones Industrial Average is only impacted by changes in the price of its underlying stocks based on supply and demand factors.

6. Dow theory postulates that movements in the Dow Industrials be confirmed by movements in the Dow Transports to validate a(n) _____ bull or bear market.

    Answer: D—Sustainable.

    Discussion: One of the six basic tenets of Dow theory is that the averages will confirm each other. Dow's original index was the Railroad Average, which has developed into today's Transportation Average. The components of the Dow Jones Industrial Average have changed quite a bit over time, but the average itself remains intact today. Combined, these two averages represented a significant portion of American business. It was Dow's view that a move upward in either average was sustainable only if the other average was also healthy and moving upward—a decline in one made continued upward movement in the other suspect.

7. True or false: The Dow Jones Industrials cannot rise if the Dow Jones Transports fall.

   Answer: False.

   Discussion: Since the components of the two averages are different (see the Media Assignment), the Dow Jones Industrial Average may be rising when the Dow Jones Transports are declining. This is referred to as *divergence* and can occur when the Industrials lead the Transports in a turn upward or if they lag the Transports in a move downward.

8. The most comprehensive barometer of the health of the NASDAQ Stock Market is the _____ Index, which is often associated with the United States' leading technology companies.

   Answer: C—NASDAQ Composite.

   Discussion: The NASDAQ Composite Index consists of all the stocks trading on the NASDAQ Stock Market. It includes shares in thousands of different companies and is significantly impacted by changes in large-cap technology stocks that dominate the index. As a result, this index is often associated with the performance of the technology sector.

9. True or false: The S&P 500 Index is the underlying index for some of the most actively traded futures and options contracts in the world.

   Answer: True.

   Discussion: The S&P 500 futures contract and the S&P 500 mini-contract are widely traded financial futures contracts that are watched worldwide. Even traders who limit themselves solely to equities trading monitor the action between the S&P futures contract and the spot price to anticipate the direction of the markets in the first few minutes. In October 2005, the Chicago Mercantile Exchange (CME) traded 902,077 S&P 500 futures contracts, 22,928,707 S&P 500 mini-contracts, and more than 2 million options contracts for both of these futures combined.

10. The S&P 500 Index is important to investors and professional money managers because it includes 500 _____.

    Answer: B—Of the largest companies trading on U.S. stock exchanges.

    Discussion: This widely followed barometer of U.S. stocks is larger than the Dow Jones Industrial Average and much more diverse. It is a benchmark that is often used to assess the performance of professional money managers and is an important index for investors to understand.

11. True or false: A sector is part of an industry group.

    Answer: False.

    Discussion: A sector is a larger, more generic group that contains industry groups. For example, the S&P Financial Sector includes banks as one industry group and insurance as a second group.

12. The technology sector includes _____ industry groups.

    Answer: C—Software services, software, and computer hardware.

    Discussion: The technology sector is the broader heading for a variety of more narrow industry groups, including software services, software, and computer hardware. Investment services, asset managers, and brokers are industry groups within the financial sector.

13. True or false: The Dow Jones Industrial Average, the NASDAQ Composite Index, and the S&P 500 are all important market barometers for investors and traders and are worth monitoring.

    Answer: True.

    Discussion: Although the Dow Jones Industrial Average has a relatively small number of companies compared to the NASDAQ Composite Index and the S&P 500 Index, it is a well-recognized index that is universally monitored. Additionally, it contains significant companies in the U.S. economy. The NASDAQ Composite Index is often associated with the technology sector, one of the most evolving areas worldwide. The S&P 500 wraps up the list with its diversity and use as a benchmark tool followed by investors and traders alike. All are important and should be monitored closely.

14. Higher-priced stocks have a _____ weighting within the Dow Jones Industrial Average.

Answer: A—Greater.

Discussion: The Dow Jones Industrial Average is a price-weighted index that gives greater weight to higher-priced stocks. The actual impact of these stocks can be reviewed in the component listing for the index that is included in this chapter.

MEDIA ASSIGNMENT

The media assignment encouraged the reader to explore the Dow Jones & Company history on its web site and review the component information detailing the four major averages the company tracks. Following the links provided, the user should initially obtain a table similar to Table 1.1 that will provide the answer about potential daily and YTD divergences.

A divergence occurs when one average is moving upward while another is moving downward. On this particular day, the Dow Jones Utility Average had a net positive change while the other three averages were negative (fourth column). We can see that the Utility Average diverged

TABLE 1.1 Dow Jones Investable Indexes

Index	Value	Net Change	% Change	YTD Change	YTD % Change
Dow Jones Industrial Average	10,686.44	−10.73	−0.1	−99.29	−0.92
Dow Jones Transportation Average	4,006.18	−53.05	−1.31	203.86	5.97
Dow Jones Utility Average	388.18	1.70	0.44	53.38	15.94
Dow Jones Composite	3,545.61	−13.29	−0.37	148.45	4.37
Indicative Dow Jones Industrial Average (U.S.)	10,686.44	−10.73	−0.1	—	—
Indicative Dow Jones Industrial Average (Europe)	10,701.70	14.69	0.14	—	—

from the other averages. In terms of YTD changes, the Industrials are slightly negative for the year while the other averages are positive (sixth column). Again there is a divergence; in this case the Industrial Average diverged from the other indexes.

The reader was also asked to determine how many components were included in each average and whether any company appeared on more than one of the first three averages. By clicking on the "Components" link in the last column, a list similar to that in Table 1.2 for the Dow Jones Utility

TABLE 1.2 Dow Jones Utility Average Components

Company Name	Ticker Symbol	Exchange	Subsector	Market Cap	Weight (%)	Price at Close
AES Corp.	AES	NYSE	Electricity	Large	2.4758	15.32
American Electric Power Co.	AEP	NYSE	Electricity	Large	5.7903	35.83
CenterPoint Energy Inc.	CNP	NYSE	Multi-Utilities	Mid	2.0879	12.92
Consolidated Edison Inc.	ED	NYSE	Electricity	Large	7.2205	44.68
Dominion Resources Inc.	D	NYSE	Electricity	Large	12.0639	74.65
Duke Energy Corp.	DUK	NYSE	Multi-Utilities	Large	4.2098	26.05
Edison International	EIX	NYSE	Electricity	Large	6.9345	42.91
Exelon Corp.	EXC	NYSE	Electricity	Large	8.1643	50.52
FirstEnergy Corp.	FE	NYSE	Electricity	Large	7.4807	46.29
NiSource Inc.	NI	NYSE	Gas Distribution	Mid	3.4745	21.50
PG&E Corp.	PCG	NYSE	Electricity	Large	5.6320	34.85
Public Svc. Enterprise Group	PEG	NYSE	Electricity	Large	9.9436	61.53
Southern Co.	SO	NYSE	Electricity	Large	5.5027	34.05
TXU Corp.	TXU	NYSE	Electricity	Large	15.7178	97.26
Williams Cos.	WMB	NYSE	Pipelines	Mid	3.3016	20.43

Average will appear in a new window. No one stock appears on all three averages (Industrial, 30 stocks; Transports, 20 stocks; and Utilities, 15 stocks).

Finally, the reader was asked to review the components of the Dow Jones Composite Average and draw a conclusion about this index. The Composite has 65 stocks and is simply a composite of the first three averages, meaning that the component stocks of the Industrials, Transports, and Utilities collectively form the Composite Average.

VOCABULARY DEFINITIONS

Average: Another term for an index—an average uses a modified divisor so that a change in value for a specific component stock due to a corporate action does not change the average itself.

Blue chip: Derived from the game of poker where blue chips carry the highest value, the term refers to large, mature, dominant companies that pay dividends. These stocks are often considered less risky than shares of smaller companies because they have less chance of running into serious financial trouble or going bankrupt.

Dividend: A corporate action for a company that involves the return of profits to investors (cash dividend). The board of directors for a company votes on whether profits should be reinvested in the firm for future growth or given to the shareholders, or a combination of both. When a dividend is issued, the value of a stock decreases by the dividend amount.

Divisor: A numeric value that incorporates the total number of index components and also makes an adjustment for various corporate activities in these underlying securities so that changes in the index reflect only price changes due to supply and demand factors.

Dow Jones Industrial Average: Charles Dow created this most widely followed index in the late nineteenth century, starting with 12 industrial companies he believed were representative of the stock market's health. Today this index includes 30 dominant companies from the financial, technology, and manufacturing sectors, among others.

Dow Jones Transportation Average: This index is the result of years of changes to the first index constructed by Charles Dow, the Dow Jones Railroad Average. It originally contained railroad company stock only, which was an important industry of Dow's time. However, today it includes 20 companies that represent various modes of transportation including railroads, airlines, trucking, and shipping.

Dow theory: Although not formalized by Charles Dow, this market viewpoint is based on six basic principles Dow published. These principles include the concept that averages should confirm each other for a bullish or bearish move to be sustainable. In other words, a rising Dow Jones Industrial Average should be confirmed by a rising Dow Jones Transportation Average. When the Transports diverge from (move counter to) the Industrials, the investor is alerted to possible weakness in the Industrials' move.

Index: A group of stocks that can be used to monitor the performance of broad markets, sectors, or industry groups. There are a variety of ways to construct an index.

Industry: The designation below *sector* for a group of companies that provide similar services or manufacture/produce similar products. The term *industry* is narrower than the term *sector*. For example, the insurance group is one of a few industries that are part of the financial sector.

Price-weighted: A method of index construction. The Dow Jones Industrial Average is a price-weighted index. See Chapter 15 for additional information on major index construction methods.

Sector: The term used to describe a group of companies that are related by a broad business focus. Examples include transportation and financials.

Stock split: A corporate action that involves the distribution of additional shares of stock to existing shareholders. This results in a decreased share price since the market value of the company remains the same pursuant to this action. A two for one (2:1) split is a common ratio. A shareholder with 100 shares of a $50 stock will now own 200 shares of a $25 stock. Companies often declare splits in order to make the share price more affordable to new investors.

Ticker symbol: Unique identifiers for stocks that trade on the exchanges. Stocks that trade on the New York Stock Exchange have symbols with one, two, or three letters. These symbols are used to view quotes, create charts, and place orders.

CHAPTER 2

The Index Market Today

SUMMARY

Investors now have the ability to view equity markets from just about any angle: by region or country, capitalization, style, sector. . . . The list is large. Although the number of indexes covered in this chapter may seem overwhelming, please keep in mind it's just the first step toward understanding what's available. As you progress through the book and put the information into use, you'll find ways to narrow your focus in a manner that suits your style.

Various entities compile and publish indexes, with the market ultimately determining which ones provide value. Equity and options exchanges, market information services, and investment firms all have compiled broad market, region, sector, and industry listings. Some of these indexes may have mechanisms to trade price movements via index options or exchange-traded funds (ETFs). If you wish to use indexes solely for monitoring the markets, then this information is not important. However, if you wish to trade, you might want to focus initially on those indexes with some trading applications.

To become a successful trader, you need to fully understand the instruments you intend to buy and sell. If you decide to trade index options, it's vital to know the characteristics and risks of that security. Be aware of trading cut-off times, expiration dates, last trade dates, and other options-specific information. If you choose to trade ETFs instead, understand the manner in which the instrument is traded (i.e., if round lots are required) as well as the correlation to the index you seek to track. It is the trader's responsibility to know about every type of security he or she trades.

QUESTIONS AND EXERCISES

1. An index measures the performance of a _____.
    A. Country's stock market.
    B. Group of stocks.
    C. Book's utility.
    D. Country's economy.

2. The components of the Dow Jones Industrial Average are determined by _____.
    A. Market capitalization.
    B. The business cycle.
    C. A committee at Dow Jones & Company.
    D. Charles Dow.

3. The _____ *effect* is the term used to explain stock price appreciation due to sudden increases in demand when it is added to an index.
    A. Index.
    B. Sudden addition.
    C. Supply-demand.
    D. S&P.

4. The S&P _____ includes the top names found in the S&P 500 Index ($SPX) and also serves as a popular underlying index for option contracts traded in the U.S. markets.
    A. Large-Cap Index ($LCI).
    B. Top Public Holdings ($ToP).
    C. Optionables ($OPT).
    D. 100 Index ($OEX).

5. Which of the following entities publish groups of indexes that are monitored by market participants?

   A. Equities exchanges.

   B. Investment firms.

   C. Options exchanges.

   D. All of the above.

6. When using index options strategies, it is important for traders to seek contracts that are _____ or _____.

   A. Liquid / inexpensive.

   B. Liquid / meet a specific need.

   C. Illiquid / inexpensive.

   D. Illiquid / long-term.

7. Determine whether each of the following is an index or security by placing an "I" or "S" in the space provided.

   A. iShares Dow Jones Real Estate _____

   B. Dow Jones Industrial Average _____

   C. PHLX Utility Sector^{SM} _____

   D. NASDAQ 100 Index _____

   E. Diamonds _____

   F. Oil Service HOLDRs _____

   G. QQQQ _____

8. True or false: Although indexes are available for the markets of countries with major economies, it is not possible to find benchmarks for those of smaller or emerging economies.

9. True or false: In addition to equities, indexes that are based on the yields for key Treasury issues are available.

10. The three exchange-traded funds (ETFs) that all traders should know and understand include _____.

    A. The Qs, diamonds, and spiders.

    B. The Qs, sapphires, and bugs.

    C. iShares, MSCI, and PowerPacks.

    D. PHLX, AMEX, and ISE.

11. True or false: Morgan Stanley Capital International (MSCI) publishes several country-specific indexes that can be traded via exchange-traded funds.

12. A unique investment vehicle that allows investors to buy and hold entire baskets of stocks in one transaction is known as _____.

    A. Holding company depositary receipts (HOLDRs).
    B. Base stock exchange transactions (BASKETs).
    C. No-load funds.
    D. Hybrids.

13. True or false: All ETFs require round lot purchases of 100 shares.

14. The streetTracks Gold Shares exchange-traded trust (GLD) is different from other indexes and ETFs because it holds _____.

    A. Gold and silver companies.
    B. Strictly gold mining companies.
    C. Gold bullion.
    D. All precious metals.

15. The _____ is one of the most active sector ETFs traded as of October 2005.

    A. Internet HOLDRs (HHH).
    B. Semiconductor HOLDRs (SMH).
    C. CBOE PowerPacks Biotech Index (PVP).
    D. iShares DJ U.S. Tech Index (IYW).

16. True or false: The Chicago Board Options Exchange (CBOE) offers options on all of the broad-based indexes.

MEDIA ASSIGNMENT

There are two media assignments for this chapter, one requiring your local Sunday paper and another requiring a computer with Internet access. The first is relatively straightforward, but will not necessarily be available to all readers. Check the business section of the Sunday paper to see if it includes an index for the major public companies in your state or region. States and regions that are highly populated business centers like California, Delaware, and those located in the northeast may not have such data. A local business journal may, however, include a table with weekly closes for companies in the region.

The next assignment involves the Internet, so again, once your computer is ready to go and you have online access, perform the following steps.

1. Type in www.standardandpoors.com into the web browser. You will use this web site to determine which company was last deleted from the S&P 500. In addition, the home page has a great deal of information about all of the S&P Indexes.

2. Look at the left column of the page and find the link to "Index Changes," which appears under the "Indices" heading. This will bring you to a page that allows a filter to be used so information about a specific index can be more easily found.

3. Using the drop-down menus provided, enter the appropriate Region ("US") and Filter Index ("S&P 500"), then click "go." Additions and deletions to the index are provided in chronological order with the most recent changes appearing first. As of January 1, 2006, what was the last company deleted from the S&P 500?

VOCABULARY LIST

Diamonds (DIA)	QQQQ
HOLDRs	Round lot
Index effect	Sin stock
iShares	SPDRs
Liquidity	Volume

SOLUTIONS

1. An index measures the performance of a _____.

   Answer: B—Group of stocks.

   Discussion: Although the performance of a country's market can be monitored through the use of country-specific indexes, an index itself measures the performance of any group of stocks. It is not limited to a broad market or region.

2. The components of the Dow Jones Industrial Average are determined by _____.

   Answer: C—A committee at Dow Jones & Company.

   Discussion: Additions and deletions to major indexes occur periodically due to corporate actions (mergers, acquisitions, etc.) or other component changes. When the Dow Jones Industrial Average is impacted by such situations, a committee at Dow Jones & Company makes changes to this widely followed index.

3. The _____ *effect* is the term used to explain stock price appreciation due to sudden increases in demand when it is added to an index.

   Answer: A—Index.

   Discussion: When a company is added to a major index, the share price will often rise. The reason for this move is that many fund companies and other institutions try to mimic the performance of these indexes. They are then forced to buy the stock, triggering a flurry of buying, commonly referred to as the *index effect*.

4. The S&P _____ includes the top names found in the S&P 500 Index ($SPX) and also serves as a popular underlying index for option contracts traded in the U.S. markets.

   Answer: D—100 Index ($OEX).

   Discussion: The S&P 500 Index ($SPX) is a capitalization-weighted index that includes the top 500 publicly traded companies. The first 100 of these companies make up another popular capitalization-weighted index, the S&P 100 Index ($OEX). The OEX was the first index to have options listed for it, and these options remain active with professional traders.

5. Which of the following entities publish groups of indexes that are monitored by market participants?

   Answer: D—All of the above (equities exchanges, investment firms, options exchanges).

   Discussion: Various entities compile and publish indexes that are used to monitor broad market, regional, sector, and industry listings. Market participants ultimately determine which of these indexes provide value via demand for data, as well as products that track them. Examples of exchange indexes include the NASDAQ 100 Index and the CBOE Internet Index. Market information services that provide indexes include Standard & Poor's (S&P 500) and the Russell Investment Group (Russell 2000). Investment firms such as Goldman Sachs (GSTI Computer Software Index) and Morgan Stanley also provide index data (MSCI Australia Index).

6. When using index options strategies, it is important for traders to seek contracts that are _____ or _____.

   Answer: B—Liquid / meet a specific need.

   Discussion: *Liquidity* is the term used to describe the depth of a particular market, meaning the number of contracts available at a given bid or offer. Greater liquidity results in narrower bid-offer spreads and greater affordability for traders. At times, however, an individual may wish to hedge the risk of an existing position. This need often supersedes the need for liquidity and would be one reason to trade less liquid options.

7. Determine whether each of the following is an index or a security by indicating "I" or "S" in the space provided.

   Answer:

   A. iShares Dow Jones Real Estate—S.
   B. Dow Jones Industrial Average—I.
   C. PHLX Utility Sector[SM]—I.
   D. NASDAQ 100 Index—I.
   E. Diamonds—S.
   F. Oil Service HOLDRs—S.
   G. QQQQ—S.

8. True or false: Although indexes are available for the markets of countries with major economies, it is not possible to find benchmarks for those of smaller or emerging economies.

   Answer: False.

   Discussion: Morgan Stanley Capital International (MSCI) has created several country-specific indexes, including those for countries that are smaller. According to the firm's web site (www.msci.com), "each MSCI Country Index captures 85% of the total country market capitalization while it accurately reflects the economic diversity of the market." A complete list of country-specific ETFs based on the MSCI sectors is available in Chapter 2.

9. True or false: In addition to equities, indexes that are based on the yields for key Treasury issues are available.

   Answer: True.

   Discussion: The Five-Year Note Index ($FVX), the Ten-Year Note Index ($TNX), and the Thirty-Year Bond Index ($TYX) are vehicles some traders use to monitor and profit from changes in interest rates. The indexes actually represent the current yield of various government notes and bonds.

10. The three exchange-traded funds (ETFs) that all traders should know and understand include _____.

    Answer: A—Qs, diamonds, and spiders.

    Discussion: The Qs (QQQQ), diamonds (DIA), and spiders, or SPDR Trust Series I (SPY) track the performance of three major U.S. equity indexes: the NASDAQ 100 ($NDX), the Dow Jones Industrial Average ($INDU), and the S&P 500 Index ($SPX), respectively. As a result, these exchange-traded funds are vital for traders who wish to capture broad-based market moves, protect a portfolio, or trade extremely liquid markets. All three are among the most heavily traded ETFs with very active underlying option contracts.

11. True or false: Morgan Stanley Capital International (MSCI) publishes several country-specific indexes that can be traded via exchange-traded funds.

    Answer: True.

    Discussion: As discussed in Question 8, ETFs on the MSCI country-specific indexes are available and listed in Chapter 2. These ETFs are part of the iShares family, and currently include 27 different country and regional groups.

12. A unique investment vehicle that allows investors to buy and hold entire baskets of stocks in one transaction is known as _____.

Answer: A—Holding company depositary receipts (HOLDRs).

Discussion: HOLDRs are a type of exchange-traded fund created by Merrill Lynch and trading on the American Stock Exchange (AMEX) in round lots. Each 100-share purchase gives the buyer ownership interest in a specific number of shares in different companies *and* the owner has the ability to break apart the investment vehicle into its individual component stocks. This is a feature unique to the HOLDRs ETF.

13. True or false: All ETFs require round lot purchases of 100 shares.

Answer: False.

Discussion: Most exchange-traded funds (ETFs) do not require that the individual buy or sell a round lot investment, which is a multiple of 100 shares. The one notable exception to this is the Merrill Lynch HOLDRs, which do require round lot transactions. The reason for this is that HOLDRs can be split up into the underlying basket of stocks represented by the ETF. Other ETFs do not afford the investor such an option.

14. The streetTracks Gold Shares exchange-traded trust (GLD) is different from other indexes and ETFs because it holds _____.

Answer: C—Gold bullion.

Discussion: There are many different indexes that track precious metals, including gold. These indexes generally include mining companies and may be limited to gold and silver or include other precious metals. The streetTracks Gold Shares exchange-traded trust (GLD) is different because it actually holds gold bullion and, as a result, is a direct proxy for the price of gold. To determine the extent to which an ETF tracks a specific commodity or index, the correlation between the two can be checked. Funds that hold oil and silver have also been launched recently.

15. The _____ is one of the most active sector ETFs traded as of October 2005.

    Answer: B—Semiconductor HOLDRs (SMH)

    Discussion: As of October 2005, SMH was one of the most active sector ETFs traded. It can be wise to periodically monitor the most actives to find highly liquid index proxies you can trade.

16. True or false: The Chicago Board Options Exchange (CBOE) offers options on all of the broad-based indexes.

    Answer: True.

    Discussion: The CBOE was the first exchange to offer equity index–based options, starting with the S&P 100 ($OEX) contracts. As time progressed, the CBOE continued to offer new index-based options products, many of which are now available on the other options exchanges.

MEDIA ASSIGNMENT

The media assignment encouraged the reader to check the local Sunday paper or a local business journal to determine if an index is published that includes major publicly traded businesses in the state or region. There may simply be weekly closes for large companies in the area or no such data available. Larger business centers may not consolidate this information.

The next assignment was to determine which company was last deleted from the S&P 500 as of January 1, 2006. By navigating through the web site and using the change filter, the user should be able to locate the S&P 500 additions/deletions page, which contains data that goes back approximately five years. On October 10, 2005, Delphi Corporation (DPH) was deleted from the S&P 500.

VOCABULARY DEFINITIONS

Diamonds (DIA): An investment vehicle that trades on the American Stock Exchange (AMEX) similarly to a stock and tracks the performance of the Dow Jones Industrial Average ($INDU). The diamonds began trading in 1998 and represent approximately $1/100$ of the value of the $INDU. Options on this security began trading in 2002.

HOLDRs: Holding Company Depositary Receipts are a unique investment vehicle that allow investors to buy and hold entire baskets of stocks in one transaction. Created by Merrill Lynch and trading on the American Stock Exchange, HOLDRs are a type of ETF that allow investors to buy and sell stocks in a particular industry, sector, or group. Unlike other ETFs, investors can elect to break apart the investment vehicle into its individual stocks. Round lot purchases of 100 shares are required for these securities.

Index effect: The term used to explain stock price appreciation due to sudden increases in demand when it is added to an index.

iShares: A family of exchange-traded funds that closely track a specific market index. Each can be bought and sold like a stock and holds a portfolio of stocks that track a specific index, such as the Dow Jones U.S. Financial Sector Index Fund (IYF).

Liquidity: The term used to describe the depth of a particular market, meaning the volume and number of shares (contracts) available at a given bid or offer. Stocks and options with high liquidity tend to have narrower spreads between the bid and offer, while less liquid securities have wider spreads.

QQQQ: An investment vehicle that trades on the AMEX similarly to a stock and tracks the performance of the NASDAQ 100 Index ($NDX). Also known as the Qs, it represents approximately $1/_{40}$ of the value of the $NDX and is one of the most actively traded investments today.

Round lot: A trade size that is a multiple of 100.

Sin stock: A public company that conducts business in fields that are deemed less socially responsible, such as tobacco companies, gaming, and alcoholic beverages.

SPDRs: An exchange-traded fund (SPY) that trades on the AMEX and holds the same companies as the S&P 500 Index ($SPX). SPDRs (pronounced "spiders") began trading in 1993 and represent approximately $1/_{100}$ of the value of the S&P 500 cash index. Options on this security began trading in 2005.

Volume: The number of shares of stock or derivatives contracts traded during a certain period of time.

CHAPTER 3

Trading the Market

SUMMARY

Whether you are interested in trading individual equities, options, or index strategies, certain market fundamentals are important to understand. These include the directional bias for the markets and the strength of that bias, how to capitalize on this information, and what to do when that bias changes. Specific tools can help you with analysis and strategy implementation, including risk graphs and price charts.

Trading bliss occurs when you're using strategies that are consistent with market direction and you are participating in moves from the strongest sectors. It's easy to imagine the opposite kind of feeling that you would experience when you have a bearish strategy in place during a bullish market, and vice versa. Chances are you'll experience both types of feelings. Let the market tell you when the situation changes rather than trying to anticipate a change, and you'll likely find yourself more in tune with the true trend.

Although we still bring biases into play when we draw trendlines, there are tools such as moving averages that can provide trend information in an unbiased manner. In addition to looking at price, traders can gain a sense of the strength of a trend by reviewing volume data. When volume expands as the trend is progressing, the move is more likely to be sustainable given the level of interest in the specific market or security. It is when volume diminishes that traders need to be wary about the strength and sustainability of the move.

QUESTIONS AND EXERCISES

1. One characteristic of bull markets is the strength of the
   _____ market as investment banks bring new companies
   public.
   A. Bond.
   B. Initial public offering (IPO).
   C. Brokerage.
   D. Transportation.

2. Three primary capitalization designations include large-cap,
   _____, and small-cap.
   A. Top.
   B. Major.
   C. XXL.
   D. Mid-cap.

3. A graphical depiction of the risk and reward associated with a trade
   is known as a(n) _____.
   A. Risk graph or risk curve.
   B. Sky's the limit.
   C. Supply-demand curve.
   D. Equity line.

4. Short selling is a bearish strategy that yields profits when prices
   _____.
   A. Move upward.
   B. Move downward.
   C. Move sideways.
   D. All of the above.

5. The _____ is one of the most widely used types of charts.
   A. Open-high-low-close (OHLC) chart.
   B. Cyclic chart.
   C. Time and distance chart.
   D. Candlestick chart.

6. A long-term bear market is often accompanied by _____ and _____.

    A. Buying / optimism.

    B. Selling / optimism.

    C. Lions / tigers.

    D. Negativity / pessimism.

7. Determine whether each of the following is an index or security by placing an "I" or "S" in the space provided.

    A. IYR   _____

    B. $INDU _____

    C. $SOX   _____

    D. QQQQ _____

    E. OIH   _____

    F. $NDX _____

    G. XLU   _____

8. True or false: A moving average is a line drawn that represents the average, or mean, price over a fixed number of days.

9. True or false: Quotes are difficult to obtain and require a subscription service or a high-volume trading account.

10. An upward trend is characterized by _____ highs and _____ lows.

    A. Lower / lower.

    B. Higher / lower.

    C. Higher / higher.

    D. Lower / higher.

11. True or false: The longer a trendline is in place, the more significant it is deemed to be.

12. An upward move that is accompanied by increasing volume is _____ and _____ the move.

   A. Bullish / concludes.

   B. Bullish / confirms.

   C. Bearish / concludes.

   D. Bearish / confirms.

13. True or false: Equity mutual funds tend to have cash inflows during bull markets.

14. A very steep upward trendline suggests _____ buying.

   A. Aggressive.

   B. Moderate.

   C. Lackluster.

   D. Fear-related.

MEDIA ASSIGNMENT

There are two media assignments for this chapter, one requiring a business newspaper such as the *Wall Street Journal* or *Investor's Business Daily*, and another requiring a computer with Internet access. Both assignments involve reviewing charts for the markets. Try to use the media platform you access most often in your analysis.

Select a major average and review a weekly chart for this average. Add trendlines and note the strength of the trend by observing how long it was and how often the line served as support or resistance. Identify the current shorter-term and longer-term trend in place. Which is more significant? It may be slightly more difficult to observe the longer-term trend if you are only able to view shorter-term charts (i.e., a daily chart). Recognize that this will also impact your analysis if you choose to use such charts in the future—limiting yourself to viewing the short-term trend may make the big picture difficult to see.

Next, add a 4-period simple moving average (SMA) and a 40-period SMA. Note that these two settings translate to a 20-day and 200-day SMA when considering the action on a daily chart. Based on the trend of these SMAs, what would you say is the short-term trend and the long-term trend? Finally, add the same SMAs to an ETF that tracks the index you were evaluating. Are the trends the same? You may not have access to this feature if completing the assignment with a newspaper.

VOCABULARY LIST

Bear market	Rally
Bull market	Resistance
Confirmation	Reversal
Correction	Risk graph
Cover (used in reference to short selling)	Short
	Short selling
Initial public offering (IPO)	Support
Long	System trading
Moving average	Trend
Nonconfirmation	Volume
Pullback	

SOLUTIONS

1. One characteristic of bull markets is the strength of the _____ market as investment banks bring new companies public.

   Answer: B—Initial public offering (IPO).

   Discussion: An initial public offering (IPO) is a new listing for a company that first comes public by making its shares available on an exchange. In order to be eligible for trading, these firms need to meet a variety of SEC and exchange requirements, including specific accounting and reporting procedures. Strong bull markets are key times for such new offerings since there is buying demand on Wall Street for both existing and new listings. Capitalizing on this general bullish bias, the price of the stock for the newly public entity will likely realize market gains sooner.

2. Three primary capitalization designations include large-cap, _____, and small-cap.

   Answer: D—Mid-cap.

   Discussion: Market capitalization, or market value, refers to the value of a company based on its stock price and shares available (float). A large-cap company has a market value range of $2.25 billion to $400 billion (average $60 billion). A mid-cap company has a range of $1 billion to $4 billion. A small-cap company has a range of $600 million to $3 billion.

3. A graphical depiction of the risk and reward associated with a trade is known as a(n) _____.

   Answer: A—Risk graph or risk curve.

   Discussion: A risk graph, or risk curve, shows the possible outcomes for a trade, including the potential profit and loss. Such graphs provide quick information about the quality of a trade from a risk-reward standpoint. It is particularly important to note positions with unlimited risk (short stock) or limited but high risk (long stock) and to have a strategy (i.e., stop-loss order placement) to minimize such risk.

4. Short selling is a bearish strategy that yields profits when prices _____.

   Answer: B—Move downward.

   Discussion: A trader who sells stock short reverses the order of buy and sell transactions by selling first. In order to do this, the trader must borrow shares from the broker holding the account and will return those shares once the shares are bought back and the position is closed. Since an individual still wants to buy low and sell high, the price of the shares of the stock must decline for the trader to realize a profit.

5. The _____ is one of the most widely used types of charts.

   Answer: A—Open-high-low-close (OHLC) chart.

   Discussion: Traders like the OHLC chart because a great deal of information is available with one quick look. Using a daily OHLC chart, the trader can easily determine the price range for the day as well as where the close took place relative to that range. A strong positive close for a stock (close near high of day) is bullish while a strong negative close (close near low of day) is bearish. Similar information for the relative placement of the open is also useful. Like other charts, the OHLC can also be used to view trend information for a series of days.

6. A long-term bear market is often accompanied by _____ and _____.

   Answer: D—Negativity / pessimism.

   Discussion: During bear markets prices are falling. What significantly increases a negative and pessimistic mind-set is the fact that investors are also losing money. When account statements arrive in the mail, individuals are reminded of the fact that some or all of their investments are declining. This direct experience is only exacerbated by media doom and gloom pronouncements. It takes some time for a trend reversal to feel real.

7. Determine whether each of the following is an index or security by placing an "I" or "S" in the space provided.

   Answer:

   A. IYR—S.

   B. $INDU—I.

   C. $SOX—I.

   D. QQQQ—S.

   E. OIH—S.

   F. $NDX—I.

   G. XLU—S.

   Discussion: The fastest way to answer this is to recognize that the symbols with the "$" represent indexes.

8. True or false: A moving average is a line drawn that represents the average, or mean, price over a fixed number of days.

   Answer: True.

   Discussion: The simple moving average is a line drawn on a price graph, connecting the average value over a number of periods. For instance, a three-day simple moving average is constructed by summing today's close with yesterday's close and the close from the day before, all divided by three. This data point will be connected to yesterday's data point which was constructed in the same manner. The result is a smooth, curved line rather than one that merely connects the daily price dots.

9. True or false: Quotes are difficult to obtain and require a subscription service or a high-volume trading account.

Answer: False.

Discussion: Many web sites (including www.Optionetics.com), newspapers, business television programs, and radio programs provide free quote information. The brokerage firm with whom you do business will also have quotes available by phone or on its web site. Generally, the quotes you receive when accessing your broker are real-time (delayed only by your connection speed), while the no-fee access points may be delayed up to 20 minutes.

10. An upward trend is characterized by _____ highs and _____ lows.

Answer: C—Higher / higher.

Discussion: The most prevalent definition of an upward trend is a trend distinguished by higher highs *and* higher lows. Although price or index levels may retrace during this move upward, buyers come in sooner with each retracement in an attempt to capitalize on the move. The opposing trend, one that is downward, is distinguished by lower highs and lower lows, with sellers coming in sooner to dispose of their shares each time a rally occurs.

11. True or false: The longer a trendline is in place, the more significant it is deemed to be.

Answer: True.

Discussion: A trendline can be drawn by connecting two price points. This trend is confirmed when the line is tested and successfully holds a third time. Although there may be more successive touches over time, this is not required for the duration of the trend to be significant. As such, trends in place for months are more significant than those in place for weeks, which are more significant than those in place for days.

12. An upward move that is accompanied by increasing volume is _____ and _____ the move.

Answer: B—Bullish / confirms.

Discussion: Volume is the fuel that drives a move, particularly on the upside. When volume increases, there is more buying demand for a security or index. This suggests all is well for the current move and is a bullish signal. Higher levels are expected (but not required). Volume is said to confirm price.

13. True or false: Equity mutual funds tend to have cash inflows during bull markets.

    Answer: True.

    Discussion: During bull markets in equities, investors watch brokerage account balances climb. This leads to a desire to more fully participate in the move by adding to existing equity mutual funds or establishing new positions. These inflows to mutual funds are generally sustained until a market reversal is under way.

14. A very steep upward trendline suggests _____ buying.

    Answer: A—Aggressive.

    Discussion: Strong movements upward with little retracement reflect aggressive buying. Individuals, for whatever reason, do not feel they can wait for a pullback and move the price higher, quickly. Such moves are generally not deemed sustainable and may reverse or become less steep.

MEDIA ASSIGNMENT

This media assignment required the reader to select a major average and review a weekly chart for it. The goal of the assignment was to identify short-term and longer-term trends using basic, core tools such as trendlines and simple moving averages (SMAs). It is important for traders to consistently pay attention to the bigger picture when evaluating trends.

The $INDU was selected as the major index for this assignment, and the ETF that will be evaluated toward the end is the AMEX diamonds (DIA). Figure 3.1 is a ProfitSource weekly chart for the index, and was selected for its flexibility in drawing trendlines and SMAs.

While not all possible trendlines were added, you can see that the Dow was recently battling between an uptrend that was valid in 2004 and a downtrend that was in place from the start of 2005—this trend had two successful holds of the trendline. The pattern you can see formed by these lines is referred to as a symmetrical triangle by technical analysts. The intermediate to longer-term trend displayed here is more sideways than anything else. Most recently, however, a sharp short-term move upward broke the downtrend line. It's slightly hasty to label this move a new longer-term advance since price still remains below February 2005 highs, but a trader can certainly monitor the situation.

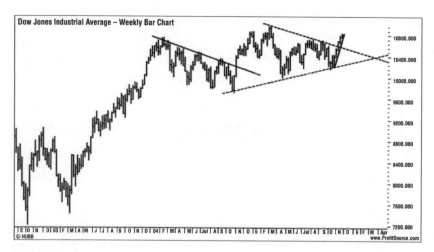

FIGURE 3.1 Weekly Chart for INDU with Trendlines (*Source:* www.ProfitSource .com)

Next, by adding a 4-period simple moving average (SMA) and a 40-period SMA, we have unbiased indicators for the short-term and long-term trend. By noting the direction of these curved lines, we not only can view trends, but we also view a chart that many market participants will view. The 20-day and 200-day SMAs are monitored by many traders and analysts. Figure 3.2 displays the weekly chart using Optionetics.com, while Figure 3.3 adds the SMAs and is from ProfitSource. The image viewed online is clearer than the image provided in text form. More detail will be available in the final chart.

The dotted 4-week SMA line on this chart is currently rising sharply with price and confirms the short-term upward trend assessment. The 40-week SMA has been relatively flat, with a recent move upward. There even appears to be a slight upward bias since early 2005—somewhat of a surprising result for traders who lived it. Regardless, while we could classify the longer-term trend as currently upward, we need to keep in mind that it does not yet reflect a strong trend. We'd like to see this average serve as support for a continued upward move.

Finally, adding these same SMA lines to the DIA, we get a clearer view of both averages. The movement in DIA is tracking movement in INDU nicely (see Figure 3.4). A trader may seek a short-term bullish trade or monitor the longer-term situation.

FIGURE 3.2   Weekly Optionetics Chart for INDU (*Source:* www.Optionetics.com)

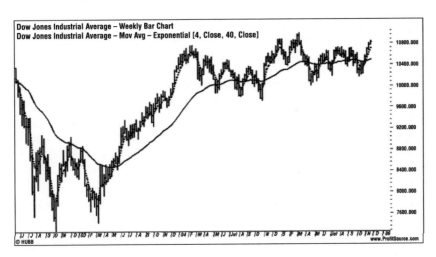

FIGURE 3.3   Weekly ProfitSource Chart for INDU (*Source:* www.ProfitSource.com)

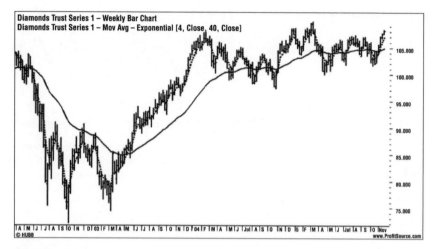

FIGURE 3.4   Weekly Chart for DIA with 4-Week and 40-Week SMAs (*Source:* www .ProfitSource.com)

VOCABULARY DEFINITIONS

Bear market: A market characterized by falling prices and money being withdrawn from the particular market that is monitored. Fear is pervasive. A technical definition includes those markets that realize a 20 percent decline or greater from a previous high.

Bull market: A market characterized by rising prices and broad investor participation in the particular market being monitored. Greed is pervasive. A technical definition includes those markets that realize a 20 percent advance or greater from a previous low.

Confirmation: In market terms, when a second indicator provides a similar signal (i.e., bullish, bearish) to an indicator being monitored.

Correction: A move lower (5 to 20 percent) during a bull market or a move higher (5 to 20 percent) during a bear market.

Cover: The term used to describe a stock transaction that closes an existing position. It is commonly used when exiting a short position (i.e., "cover the short stock").

Initial public offering (IPO): The first shares available when a private company goes public and makes its stock available on an exchange.

Long: A term used to describe an ownership position in a stock, option, or other investment. Being long is a bullish strategy that profits when the price of the asset moves higher.

Moving average: A line constructed on a chart by calculating the cumulative total for price closes over a certain period of time, then dividing that value by the number of periods used (simple average). A three-day moving average line, for example, is then constructed by taking the average value of the closes over the past three days and dividing it by 3.

Nonconfirmation: In market terms, when a second indicator provides the opposing signal (i.e., bullish, bearish) to an indicator being monitored. This is also referred to as *divergence.*

Pullback: A move of 5 percent or less to the downside during a bull market or a move 5 percent or less to the upside during a bear market. Such a move occurs during a sustained trend, in the opposite direction of that trend.

Rally: A strong upward movement in a security after a decline or sideways trending period that is accompanied by high volume.

Resistance: A ceiling above the current price of a stock where selling pressure enters the market.

Reversal: A sudden and sustained change in the direction of price that follows a downward or upward trend.

Risk graph: A graphical depiction of the risk and reward associated with a trade. It shows the possible outcomes, including the potential profit and loss, or risk. Also called a risk curve.

Short: A bearish position that profits from a move lower in the stock. A short seller borrows shares from the broker and sells them at the current market price. The shares are eventually bought back and returned to the broker.

Short selling: The process of selling shares in the market by first borrowing those shares from a broker. When initiating a position through a short sale, the trader must eventually purchase the shares in the market so they can be returned to the broker. Short selling essentially reverses the normal order of a stock transaction (buy to initiate the position, sell to close the position).

Support: A floor below the current price of a stock where buyers enter the market.

System trading: A trade approach that includes specific rules for trade entry and exit. Flexibility is built into this method by varying the indicators and speed used to obtain signals or by adding filters (additional requirements).

Trend: A prolonged period during which a stock's price moves in one direction. If the market is moving gradually higher and setting a series of higher highs and higher lows, it is said to be in an uptrend. When prices are moving gradually lower and setting a series of lower highs and lower lows, it is said to be in a downtrend.

Volume: The number of shares of stock (or option contracts) traded during a certain period of time; daily volume is a common measurement.

Understanding Options

SUMMARY

In Chapter 4, we transition to a new type of security that enables us to trade moves on a number of indexes: options. Index options and equity options on exchange-traded funds (ETF) provide individuals with two additional ways to create an index-based trading plan. These securities derive their value from, among other factors, the level or price of the underlying index or security. Traders can take advantage of options strategies that benefit from upward or downward movement in the underlying security while also being able to employ strategies that capitalize on sideways movement.

Options for the U.S. equity market have been in existence for more than 30 years. Currently there are six exchanges that facilitate trading in these securities. In 2005 these markets were extremely active with volume clearly exceeding expectations of the original options traders in 1973. New products continue to make the options market dynamic.

There are two types of options: calls and puts. A long call gives the buyer the right, but not the obligation, to call away or purchase the underlying security at a set price (strike price) by a set date (expiration date). A long put gives the buyer the right, but not the obligation, to put or sell the underlying security at a set price (strike price) by a set date (expiration date). These are the most basic definitions for options; these securities can also be sold short or used in different combinations that will create obligations or minimize risk, depending on the use. If you are new to these securities, we suggest you read earlier texts on the subject such as *The Options Course* and *The Volatility Course*, as well as the Options Clearing Corporation (OCC) publication *Characteristics and Risks of Standardized Options*.

The option's premium, or price, is determined by the price of the underlying security relative to the option type and strike price, along with four other primary determinants. These include (1) time to expiration, (2) volatility of the underlying, (3) dividends issued by the underlying during the life of the option, and (4) interest rates. It is extremely important to understand the impact each of these will have on the value of the option when it is purchased, when you wish to sell it, and at expiration.

Although many traders simply buy and sell options (not necessarily in that order), they may also use these securities to exercise rights in order to take possession of (or sell) the underlying security. Option traders must understand the risks associated with short option positions and be prepared for possible option assignment, as conditions warrant. Since the seller has an obligation and not a right, the only control the trader has is to offset a position by covering a short in order to gain relief from the contract obligation. Recognizing conditions that will impact assignment is an important skill for option writers.

Option traders have many choices available to them in terms of both the underlying security eligible for trading as well as the strategies that can be employed to capitalize on specific moves in the underlying. As with any security, however, it is critical that the trader understand what impacts an option's value and what risks and obligations are associated with the position. As with equity and ETF positions, risk graphs provide invaluable information to the options trader.

QUESTIONS AND EXERCISES

1. The Options Clearing Corporation (OCC) was created as the clearing agent for _____ United States–based options exchanges and still performs that role today.

    A. All.
    B. Most.
    C. Some.
    D. No.

2. The two types of options include _____ and _____, with the former giving the owner the right to buy the underlying security.
   A. Sells / buys.
   B. Calls / puts.
   C. Buys / sells.
   D. Puts / calls.

3. _____ stands for long-term equity anticipation securities, which have longer expiration periods than regular option contracts.
   A. L-TEAS.
   B. LTs.
   C. "Long options."
   D. LEAPS.

4. The difference between the bid and the ask is known as the _____.
   A. Specialist's sweet spot.
   B. Bi-Sk.
   C. Spread.
   D. Skew.

5. The _____ is another term used for the cost of an option.
   A For the money.
   B. Delta.
   C. Premium.
   D. Alpha.

6. Match the term with its definition by placing the proper number in the space provided. This particular exercise is geared toward call options.
   A. Intrinsic value ____ 1. Stock price approximately = strike price.
   B. Time value ____ 2. Stock price – call strike price.
   C. In-the-money ____ 3. Stock price > call strike price.
   D. At-the-money ____ 4. Stock price < call strike price.
   E. Out-of-the-money ____ 5. Call option price + strike price – stock price.

7. True or false: The Options Industry Council (OIC) is in place to protect floor traders' and market makers' rights.

8. An example of a covered call strategy includes the purchase of _____ and the simultaneous sale of _____.
   A. 100 shares of XYZ stock / 1 XYZ call option.
   B. 1 XYZ call / 1 XYZ put.
   C. 100 shares of XYZ stock / 1 XYZ put option.
   D. 1 XYZ call / 1 XYZ call.

9. True or false: Time value decreases at an accelerating rate.

10. Place a checkmark next to the factors that impact an option's price or premium.
    A. Time to expiration   _____
    B. Lunar cycle   _____
    C. Price of underlying   _____
    D. Strike price   _____
    E. Broker's mark-up   _____
    F. Volatility of underlying   _____
    G. Propulsion factor   _____

11. True or false: Time is a negligible factor in determining an option's value.

12. True or false: "Buying to open" an option contract creates a debit in a trader's account, and "selling to open" an option contract creates a credit in a trader's account.

13. In order to offset (close) an open option position, a trader should sell _____.
    A. 100 shares of the underlying stock.
    B. An equal number of contracts of the exact same option contract.
    C. 100 of the exact same option contract.
    D. None of the above.

14. The OCC _____ matches or assigns buyers and sellers.
    A. Occasionally.
    B. Negatively.
    C. Randomly.
    D. Expeditiously.

15. The probability of assignment increases as the time value of an option drops below 0.25 and the option moves _____.
    A. Out-of-the-money.
    B. In-the-money.
    C. In-to-volatility.
    D. Out-of-volatility.

16. True or false: An American-style option can only be exercised at expiration.

17. There are two different types of option settlement: _____ and _____.
    A. Cash-settled / physical delivery.
    B. Specialist settled / physical delivery.
    C. Cash only / pizza delivery.
    D. Not applicable / cash-settled.

18. An option with a premium of $2 and a multiplier of 100 would cost a trader _____.
    A. $2.
    B. $100.
    C. $200 ($2 × 100).
    D. Their pride (and that's too high a price).

19. True or false: Open interest is the number of media venues that publish daily prices for a particular option.

MEDIA ASSIGNMENT

There is one media assignment for this chapter that requires a computer with Internet access. Once you are logged in, type www.optionetics.com into the web browser. This will take you to the Optionetics web site, where you will be able to bring up option chains and detailed quotes, among other option specific data. Bring up an option chain for any widely known stock (no indexes or ETFs) by entering the stock symbol in the "quotes/options" field and selecting "Chain" in the drop-down menu immediately to the right of this field. Select "GO" when you are ready.

Identify and write down a near month call option (including symbol) and a near month put option (including symbol) for contracts that are approximately at-the-money. Next, write down the premium for each of these contracts, as well as the cost of one contract. Finally determine the intrinsic value and the time value (also called *extrinsic value*) for each of these contracts.

Repeat the exercise using the same underlying stock for both a call and a put option that have more than two months to expiration. What did you note about the time value for the near month contracts? What about the intrinsic value?

VOCABULARY LIST

Ask	Clearing agent or clearinghouse
Assignment	Commission
At-the-money	Delivery
Auto-exercise	Derivatives
Bid	Early exercise
Black-Scholes Model	Exercise
Breakeven	Exercise settlement amount
Call	Exercise settlement value
Cash settlement	Futures
Chicago Board Options Exchange (CBOE)	In-the-money
	Intrinsic value

Long-term equity anticipation securities (LEAPS)

Moneyness

Multiplier

Offer

Open interest

Options Clearing Corporation (OCC)

Options Industry Council (OIC)

Out-of-the-money

Package

Physical delivery settlement

Premium

Put

Risk graph

Securities and Exchange Commission (SEC)

Spread

Time decay

Wasting asset

Writer

SOLUTIONS

1. The Options Clearing Corporation (OCC) was created as the clearing agent for _____ United States–based options exchanges and still performs that role today.

   Answer: A—All.

   Discussion: The OCC began clearing options roughly two years after the founding of the first United States–based options exchange in Chicago—the Chicago Board Options Exchange (CBOE). This clearing entity was approved by the Securities and Exchange Commission (SEC) and remains the sole clearing group for the standardized index and equity options described in this chapter.

2. The two types of options include _____ and _____, with the former giving the owner the right to buy the underlying security.

   Answer: B—Calls / puts.

   Discussion: A call option gives the buyer the right, but not the obligation, to buy or call the underlying asset at a specific price (strike price) for a specific period of time (expiration date). A put option gives the buyer the right, but not the obligation, to sell or put the underlying asset at a specific price (strike price) for a specific period of time (expiration date).

3. _____ stands for long-term equity anticipation securities, which have longer expiration periods than regular option contracts.

   Answer: D—LEAPS.

   Discussion: The acronym used for these long-term option contracts that generally have expirations of nine months or greater is LEAPS. These securities typically expire in January; however, some index options have LEAPS with December expirations. A LEAPS eventually becomes a regular option with the same characteristics.

4. The difference between the bid and the ask is known as the _____.

   Answer: C—Spread.

   Discussion: The spread is the difference between the bid and the ask and reflects the specialist's or market maker's premium to accept the risk of making a market for a particular security. Greater liquidity for a security is reflected by a narrower spread.

5. The _____ is another term used for the cost of an option.

   Answer: C—Premium.

   Discussion: The premium is the amount of cash that an option buyer pays to an option seller. The total cost of the option contract is the premium multiplied by the option multiplier (usually 100).

6. Match the term with its definition by placing the proper number in the space provided. This particular exercise is geared toward call options.

   Answer:

   A. Intrinsic value—2. Stock price – call strike price.
   B. Time value—5. Call option price + strike price – stock price.
   C. In-the-money—3. Stock price > call strike price.
   D. At-the-money—1. Stock price approximately = strike price.
   E. Out-of-the-money—4. Stock price < call strike price.

7. True or false: The Options Industry Council (OIC) is in place to protect floor traders' and market makers' rights.

   Answer: False.

   Discussion: The OIC is a nonprofit association created to educate the investing public and brokers about the benefits and risks of exchange-traded options. It is comprised of five options exchanges and NYSE ARCA, the owner of the sixth options exchange (PCX).

8. An example of a covered call strategy includes the purchase of _____ and the simultaneous sale of _____.

   Answer: A—100 shares of XYZ stock / 1 XYZ call option.

   Discussion: This options strategy includes a base position of 100 shares of stock. A call option for the underlying stock is sold, thus obligating the trader to sell the 100 shares at the strike price, usually for a profit. The call is then covered by the shares of stock. If the stock is below the strike price at the time of expiration, the premium for the call is kept and another call option can be sold against the 100 shares.

9. True or false: Time value decreases at an accelerating rate.

   Answer: True.

   Discussion: The greater the amount of time value in the option, the less likely the option will be exercised. But time value falls as time passes—this occurs at an accelerating rate. As a result, an option with only one month of life remaining will see time value erode faster than an options contract with six months remaining until it expires. At expiration, time value will equal zero.

10. Place a checkmark next to the factors that impact an option's price or premium:

    Answer:

    A. Time to expiration—Yes.

    B. Lunar cycle—No.

    C. Price of underlying—Yes.

    D. Strike price—Yes.

    E. Broker's mark-up—No.

    F. Volatility of underlying—Yes.

    G. Propulsion factor—No.

11. True or false: Time is a negligible factor in determining an option's value.

    Answer: False.

    Discussion: Time is the second most important factor, after the price of the underlying, in an option's price. The more time to expiration, the greater the value of the option.

12. True or false: "Buying to open" an option contract creates a debit in a trader's account, and "selling to open" an option contract creates a credit in a trader's account.

   Answer: True.

   Discussion: When a trader initiates a long option position (call or put), the debit to the account is the value of the options premium. When initiating a short option position (call or put), the premium amount enters the account as a credit. This is similar to a stock short sale; however, the margin requirements for these two types of positions are different.

13. In order to offset (close) an open option position, a trader should sell _____.

   Answer: B—An equal number of contracts of the exact same option contract.

   Discussion: Options trades include (1) opening transactions to establish a new position and (2) offsetting, closing transactions to close the position. Since option contracts are created by supply and demand—rather than maintaining a fixed float like stocks—these offsetting transactions result in a net zero position for the trader while allowing proper OCC accounting for outstanding contracts.

14. The OCC _____ matches or assigns buyers and sellers.

   Answer: C—Randomly.

   Discussion: The OCC randomly performs assignments to member brokers, who then complete assignments across their customer accounts. Typically, the broker's method for assignment is also random.

15. The probability of assignment increases as the time value of an option drops below 0.25 and the option moves _____.

   Answer: B—In-the-money.

   Discussion: Exercise generally takes place only with in-the-money (ITM) options. A call option that has a strike price below the price of the underlying index is ITM. If an ETF is currently trading near $55.00, the March 50 call options will have an intrinsic value of $5.00 because the option buyer can exercise the option, buy shares for $50.00, immediately sell them in the market for $55.00, and realize a $5.00 profit. A put option, on the other hand, will be ITM when the stock price is below the strike price.

16. True or false: An American-style option can only be exercised at expiration.

    Answer: False.

    Discussion: The option style that can only be exercised at expiration is a European-style contract. American-style options can be exercised at any time up to the cut-off on the business day before expiration.

17. There are two different types of option settlement: _____ and _____.

    Answer: A—Cash-settled / physical delivery.

    Discussion: Equity options have settlement that includes physical delivery. A call option holder has the right to receive delivery of a physical asset—a stock—while the owner of a put stock option has the right to sell 100 shares of stock per options contract. Exchange-traded funds also settle for the physical delivery of shares. Index options do not involve the physical delivery of an asset because it is not possible to buy and sell an index. Instead, cash-settled calls and puts give the owner the right to receive cash. In order to determine how much, if any, cash the option holder is entitled to receive, one must consider the relationship between the exercise settlement value and the strike price of the option.

18. An option with a premium of $2 and a multiplier of 100 would cost a trader _____.

    Answer: C—$200 ($2 × 100).

    Discussion: The option premium ($2) times the option multiplier (100) equals the amount paid by an option buyer, without commissions. Occasionally, stocks that have undergone certain corporate actions require adjustments to existing options that result in a multiplier that is different from 100. Such options are appropriately known as "adjusted options" and generally have a different option root symbol.

19. True or false: Open interest is the number of media venues that publish daily prices for a particular option.

    Answer: False.

    Discussion: Open interest is the number of outstanding contracts available for a specific option based on the opening and closing transactions for the security. An updated open interest value is generally available the next trading day. Open interest is different from the number of contracts traded in a day (volume) since it makes a net adjustment for contracts that are closed.

MEDIA ASSIGNMENT

This media assignment required the reader to look up an option chain, determine which contracts were near term and at-the-money, and calculate the intrinsic and extrinsic value of the option premium. The first step was to bring up the Optionetics.com web site. In the example here, the symbol for Microsoft Corporation (MSFT) was entered in the "quotes/options" field and the "Chain" option was selected in the drop-down menu immediately to the right of this field. This is shown in Figure 4.1.

When "GO" in the quotes/options section is selected, a full list of call and put options for various months appears for MSFT. Figure 4.2 shows the quote information for the underlying security, as well as the option information for the near month, at-the-money call and put. A longer list of options should be displayed when you select "GO."

This chain was obtained in late November 2005 after the expiration of November options. As a result, the near month option is now December. We'll look at options in December for the first part of this exercise. Also, since the price of the underlying security at the time of this writing was $27.55, we look down the list of strike prices for December and note the closest strike price to this value is $27.50.

FIGURE 4.1 Retrieving an Option Chain from the Optionetics Web Site (*Source:* www.Optionetics.com)

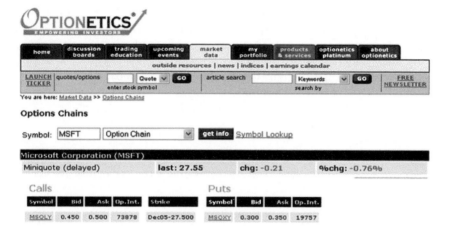

FIGURE 4.2 Near Month At-the-Money Options for Microsoft (MSFT) (*Source:* www.Optionetics.com)

The near month call option is MSQLY, the December 27.50 call contract; and the near month put option is MSQXY, the December 27.50 put contract. The premium for a long call buyer is the current ask for the contract, or $0.50, as seen in Figure 4.2. The premium for a long put buyer is the current ask for MSQXY, or $0.35.

The intrinsic value is the difference between the strike price and the underlying asset's price. For a call option, it is the price of the underlying minus the call strike price, while for a put option it is the put strike price minus the price of the underlying. In the MSFT example, the call intrinsic value is calculated as follows:

27.55 (price of the underlying) – 27.50 (call strike price) = 0.05

The put intrinsic value is as follows:

27.50 (put strike price) – 27.55 (price of the underlying) = –0.05 = 0

The intrinsic value is not negative but rather zero when the calculation yields a negative value.

The extrinsic or time value for these contracts is the premium amount less any intrinsic value. In the example for MSFT, the extrinsic call value is the call premium minus the call intrinsic value, and the extrinsic put value is the put premium minus the put intrinsic value. The following two results are calculated:

$$0.55 \text{ (call premium)} - 0.05 \text{ (call intrinsic value)} = 0.50$$

$$0.35 \text{ (put premium)} - 0.00 \text{ (put intrinsic value)} = 0.35$$

The more complete formula is

Call premium − (price of the underlying − call strike price)

When you repeat the exercise using the same underlying stock for both a call and put option that have more than two months to expiration, an April 27.50 call (symbol MSQDY) and an April 27.50 put (symbol MSQPY) are found. The time value for the near month contracts will be less than the time value for the April contracts since an additional four months is available for the underlying to reach that trader's target price. The intrinsic value is the amount the contract is in-the-money, and it remains the same for both expiration months. The difference in premiums is limited to the option's extrinsic value.

VOCABULARY DEFINITIONS

Ask: The lowest price of a specific market that market makers, floor brokers, or specialists are willing to sell at. Also see Offer.

Assignment: The receipt of an exercise notice by an options writer that requires him to sell (in the case of a call) or purchase (in the case of a put) the underlying security at the specified strike price.

At-the-money: When the strike price of an option is the same as, or close to, the price of the underlying security. Also referred to as *near-the-money*.

Auto-exercise: An exercise (physical or cash, as applicable) performed by the OCC at expiration when the value of the option is $0.25 or more for physical settlement or $0.01 or more for cash settlement on the expiration date. The OCC assumes the contract holder did not want an option with value to expire worthless.

Bid: An indication by an investor, a trader, or a dealer of a willingness to buy a security; the price at which an investor can sell to a broker-dealer.

Black-Scholes Model: An analytical model that can determine the fair market value of options. It is the most widely used options-pricing model used by traders today.

Breakeven: The point at which a trade yields no profit or loss.

Call: (1) An option contract giving the holder the right, but not the obligation, to buy a specified amount of an underlying security at a specified price within a specified time. (2) The act of exercising a call option.

Cash settlement: An obligation that is met via cash when the underlying asset does not physically exist, such as an equity index.

Chicago Board Options Exchange (CBOE): (Pronounced "C-Bow") One of the largest options exchanges in the United States.

Clearing agent or clearinghouse: An institution that ensures the payment and delivery of stock between investment dealers in a timely, cost-efficient manner.

Commission: The fee paid to a broker to execute buy and sell orders; this can be a fixed rate or a percentage of the transaction's value.

Delivery: The manner in which a right or obligation is met for option contracts. Index options have cash delivery while equity options have physical delivery.

Derivatives: Financial instruments whose value is based on the market value of an underlying asset such as stocks, bonds, or a commodity. Examples of derivatives are futures contracts and options. Derivatives are generally used by institutional investors to increase overall portfolio return or to hedge portfolio risk.

Early exercise: An exercise that occurs prior to expiration.

Exercise: To implement the right of the holder of an option to buy (in the case of a call) or sell (in the case of a put) the underlying security. When you exercise an option, you carry out the terms of an option contract.

Exercise settlement amount: The difference between the exercise price and the exercise settlement value of an index on the day the exercise notice is tendered, multiplied by the multiplier (100).

Exercise settlement value: The value of the index at the time of expiration.

Futures: A term used to designate all contracts covering the purchase and sale of financial instruments or physical commodities for future delivery on a commodity futures exchange.

In-the-money: An option that, if exercised, would generate a profit is referred to as *in-the-money*. For example, when a stock price is $50, a call option with a strike price of $40 is considered in-the-money.

Intrinsic value: The difference between the strike price and the underlying asset's price. For a call option, it is the price of the underlying minus the call strike price, while for a put option it is the put strike price minus the price of the underlying.

Long-term equity anticipation securities (LEAPS): Long-term stock or index options. LEAPS, like all options, are available in two types, calls and puts, with expiration dates up to three years in the future.

Moneyness: The relationship between the price of the underlying asset and the strike price of the option.

Multiplier: The option component that is used to determine the net cost of the security; it is typically 100.

Offer (ask): An indication by a trader or a dealer of a willingness to sell a security; the price at which an investor can buy from a broker-dealer.

Open interest: The number of outstanding contracts in the exchange market or in a particular series; these contracts have been opened but not yet closed.

Options Clearing Corporation (OCC): The clearing agent for all United States–based options exchanges.

Options Industry Council (OIC): A nonprofit association created to educate the investing public and brokers about the benefits and risks of exchange-traded options.

Out-of-the-money: An option that, if exercised, would generate a loss is referred to as *out-of-the-money*. For example, when a stock price is $50, a call option with a strike price of $55 is considered out-of-the-money.

Package: The underlying asset or combination of assets from which an option is derived. Typically, the option package for an equity option is 100 shares of one stock.

Physical delivery settlement: An obligation that is met via delivery of an asset, such as stock or an exchange-traded fund.

Premium: The amount of cash that an option buyer pays to an option seller to purchase an option. In contrast, the amount of credit an option seller receives when shorting an option.

Put: (1) An option contract giving the owner the right, but not the obligation, to sell a specified amount of an underlying security at a specified price within a specified time. (2) The act of exercising a put option.

Risk graph: Also known as risk curve, a risk graph is a graphical depiction of the risk and reward associated with a trade. These graphs show the possible outcomes for a trade, including the potential profit and loss, and provide quick information about the quality of a trade from a risk/reward standpoint.

Securities and Exchange Commission (SEC): A commission created by Congress to regulate the securities markets and protect investors. It is composed of five commissioners appointed by the President of the United States and approved by the Senate. The SEC enforces, among other acts, the Securities Act of 1933, the Securities Exchange Act of 1934, the Trust Indenture Act of 1939, the Investment Company Act of 1940, and the Investment Advisers Act of 1940.

Spread: The difference between the bid and the offer for a security.

Time decay: The option characteristic whereby the asset loses value as time progresses. The price component related to this phenomenon is referred to as *theta*. (See wasting asset.)

Wasting asset: An asset that has a limited life and thus decreases in value (depreciates) over time. An option contract is a wasting asset because the chance of a favorable move in the underlying stock diminishes as the contract approaches expiration, therefore reducing its value.

Writer: An individual who sells an option as an opening transaction.

Basic Strategies Using Call Options

SUMMARY

Chapter 5 takes the reader from a basic call strategy to those that blend primarily calls and stock to adjust risk. Strategies that limit risk, even when the reward is reduced, are preferred to those with higher to unlimited risks. Always assess the ultimate risk/reward picture for a potential trade prior to establishing it. Although a risk graph provides a nice, fast visual representation of this information, the trader minimally must calculate these values by hand to determine if the risk is within his or her trading constraints and whether the risk/reward ratio is acceptable.

Quite a few trade strategies are examined in this chapter. They include the long call, short call, bear call spread, covered call, call calendar spread, and bull call spread. A quick summary of these strategies is provided in Table 5.1. When evaluating a strategy given a certain market outlook (i.e., bullish, neutral), the trader should also consider other strategies that benefit from a similar outlook while improving the risk/reward prospects.

A bear call spread is a limited-risk credit spread (money comes into the account when the trade is established) that can be used when a trader is bearish to neutral on a security. The reward is limited to the credit received. In a low-volatility environment (low premium), the

TABLE 5.1 Call Strategy Matrix

Strategy	Position	Market Conditions	Risk/ Reward	Acceptable
Long call	Long call	Bullish	Limited/ unlimited	Yes
Short call	Short call	Bearish, neutral	Unlimited/ limited	No
Bear call spread	Long higher strike, short lower strike (1:1)	Bearish, neutral	Limited/ limited	Yes*
Bull call spread	Long lower strike, short higher strike (1:1)	Bullish	Limited/ limited	Yes
Call calendar spread	Long longer term, short shorter term (1:1)	Neutral to bullish	Limited/ limited	Yes
Covered call	Long stock, short call (100 shares per 1 call)	Short-term neutral, Long-term bullish	Limited (high)/ limited	Yes*

*The strategy has risk that is limited and is therefore acceptable; however, a different strategy may better serve the trader's outlook from a risk/reward scenario.

trader may want to consider a bear put spread that is established for a debit. Such a trade also has limited risk, but in this case the spread is relatively inexpensive to establish and the reward potentially greater than with the bear call credit spread. Market outlook and conditions, as well as the trader's risk tolerance, are all factors that impact strategy selection.

Not all traders have approval to use all option strategies. The type of strategies allowed is dictated by the account option level, which is determined by the compliance and risk departments of the brokerage firm holding the account. Factors impacting the account level include the account type, the experience of all account holders, and the financial standing of all account holders. While such measures are intended to limit losses for less experienced traders or those with more limited access to funds, it is still possible for substantial losses to occur in options trading. A strategist must always understand the risks for trades established and actively manage that risk.

QUESTIONS AND EXERCISES

1. An out-of-the-money strike call option has greater _____ due to the lower premium paid for the security; however, there is a greater chance such an option will expire worthless.
   A. Possibilities.
   B. Time value.
   C. Leverage.
   D. Success rates.

2. True or false: Option trades can have stop-losses that are based on the market price for the option or the market price for the underlying security.

3. A naked short call has _____ risk and _____ reward since the underlying security can technically rise without limit.
   A. Unlimited / limited.
   B. Unlimited / unlimited.
   C. Limited / unlimited.
   D. Great / greater.

4. A bear call spread is appropriate when the strategist is bearish or _____ on the underlying asset.
   A. Bullish.
   B. Confident.
   C. Overconfident.
   D. Neutral.

5. A bear call spread with a higher-strike long call and lower-strike short call reaches its maximum profit potential once the price of the underlying reaches the _____ strike price (Hint: What is the outlook for the trader?)
   A. Maximum.
   B. Lower.
   C. Spread.
   D. Higher.

6. True or false: Any option strategy that makes use of stock for an underlying can also make use of an ETF or index.

7. Match the strategy with the security outlook.

    A. Long call   _____   1. Bearish.

    B. Bear call spread   _____   2. Generally neutral, then

    C. Long put   bullish.

    D. Call calendar spread   _____   3. Bullish.

                                 _____   4. Bearish to neutral.

8. Match the spread with the option strike image and identify a strategy example for A and B.

    A. Horizontal spread   _____   Strategy: _____

    B. Vertical spread   _____   Strategy: _____

    C. Diagonal spread   _____

Jan.	Feb.	Mar.
50	50	50
55	55	55
60	60	60

Spread #1

Jan.	Feb.	Mar.
50	50	50
55	55	55
60	60	60

Spread #2

Jan.	Feb.	Mar.
50	50	50
55	55	55
60	60	60

Spread #3

9. Assuming a call calendar spread has reached the first expiration month and the short call has expired worthless, and given a bullish outlook for the security, the strategist can (a) hold the remaining long call to sell it at an opportune time, or (b) _____ to create a bull call spread.

    A. Sell another higher-strike call.

    B. Buy shares of stock.

    C. Buy a protective put.

    D. Roll out the remaining option.

10. True or false: A bull call spread is a debit spread created by purchasing a lower-strike call and simultaneously selling a higher-strike call on the same underlying with the same expiration date.

11. _____ is a type of form required for a customer wishing to add options trading to a brokerage account.

    A. Option Strategy Form.

    B. Consent Form.

    C. Option Approval Form.

    D. Guaranteed No-Loss Form.

12. True or false: The more complicated the strategy, the lower the option approval required.

13. True or false: In the event a trader does not have access to option analysis software, it is acceptable for the trader to enter a trade without calculating the risk and reward.

MEDIA ASSIGNMENT

There is one, two-part media assignment for this chapter that can be completed using any media source that provides sufficient information for you to identify an intermediate-term outlook for the NASDAQ 100 Index Trust (QQQQ). We are considering a one- to three-month outlook when we indicate "intermediate-term." Newspapers and online resources are both suitable for this exercise.

The reader should perform an analysis on QQQQ and indicate whether the outlook is bullish, bearish, or neutral for the ETF. Identify a strategy from this chapter that is consistent with your outlook to capitalize on current market conditions. Identify the conditions for the maximum risk to occur for the position (i.e., above the higher strike).

Finally, assume QQQQ options are available in strike prices up to $10 below and $10 above the current price for the ETF, in $1 increments (i.e., if QQQQ is currently at $40, there are options available at 30, 31, 32, . . . , 48, 49, 50). Also assume that QQQQ options are available in March, June, September, and December, as well as the current and next expiration month. Identify a specific position using the strategy obtained in the first part of this exercise. If you have easy access to quotes, also identify the net debit or credit for the position.

VOCABULARY LIST

Bear put spread	Naked call
Bull call spread	Protective put
Calendar spread	Rolling
Collar spread	Stop-loss
Compliance department	Trading level
Diagonal spread	Vertical spread
Horizontal spread	

SOLUTIONS

1. An out-of-the-money strike call option has greater _____ due to the lower premium paid for the security; however, there is a greater chance such an option will expire worthless.

   Answer: C—Leverage.

   Discussion: The best answer is leverage. Since higher-strike call premiums are less than those premiums for calls with lower strikes, an out-of-the-money call achieves greater leverage when the underlying closes above the strike price by expiration. As an example, suppose stock XYZ is trading at $52. Trader A purchases a 50 strike call for $3 and Trader B purchases a 55 strike call for $0.80. If the stock closes at $57 at expiration, then trader A's return is 133 percent (profit of $4 for an investment of $3) and Trader B's return is 150 percent. It is important to note, however, that there is a minimum level the underlying must reach in order for the leverage to be effective. These options have a greater chance of expiring worthless. Using our example, stock XYZ can trade from approximately $50.25 to $55 and still retain value for Trader A, while Trader B would lose the entire investment.

2. True or false: Option trades can have stop-losses that are based on the market price for the option or the market price for the underlying security.

   Answer: True.

   Discussion: Although the trader may not be able to physically place two orders for one position, a mental stop-loss can be noted that is based on a threshold price for the option itself, or for the underlying security. A stop-loss based on the underlying security may be entered as a conditional order, depending on the order capabilities of your broker. A conditional order is one in which the price of one security triggers an order for another security.

3. A naked short call has _____ risk and _____ reward since the underlying security can technically rise without limit.

   Answer: A—Unlimited / limited.

   Discussion: Although it is hard to picture, a stock can theoretically rise indefinitely, without limit. As a result, any trader who is short a stock or has an obligation that would create a short stock position (such as a naked short call) has risk without limit. The maximum reward for a naked short call writer is the premium received when the position is established.

4. A bear call spread is appropriate when the strategist is bearish or _____ on the underlying asset.

   Answer: D—Neutral.

   Discussion: A bear call spread is constructed with a short lower-strike price call and a long higher-strike price call. There are three possible regions in which the stock can close relative to these two strike prices: above both strike prices, between them, and below both strike prices. When the stock is above both strike prices the two calls have both appreciated in value if assigned; the trader is obligated to sell shares at the lower strike and can purchase them back at the higher strike. This bullish move for the stock results in a "sell low, buy high" trade with a maximum loss for the trader. Since the trade is created for a credit, sideways movement (neutral) in the stock results in a reduced value in the combined position as time decay negatively impacts the premium for both calls. While not optimal, the trade can result in minimum profits or minimum losses depending on where price closes relative to the two strikes. Finally, the optimal situation occurs when the stock closes below both strike prices (bearish) and the calls expire worthless. This is the maximum profit area.

5. A bear call spread with a higher-strike long call and lower-strike short call reaches its maximum profit potential once the price of the underlying reaches the _____ strike price (Hint: What is the outlook for the trader?)

   Answer: B—Lower.

   Discussion: When the stock closes at the same value as the lower strike price, both options expire worthless. The trader keeps the initial credit, which is the maximum profit for the trade. (See discussion in answer 4.)

6. True or false: Any option strategy that makes use of stock for an underlying can also make use of an ETF or index.

   Answer: False.

   Discussion: Since an index is not a security that can be purchased, strategies that combine shares and options are not possible. Such strategies can be implemented with an ETF providing the ETF has options associated with it.

7. Match the strategy with the security outlook.

   Answer:

   A. Long call—3. Bullish.

   B. Bear call spread—4. Bearish to neutral.

   C. Long put—1. Bearish.

   D. Call calendar spread—2. Generally neutral, then bullish.

   Discussion: See each strategy's description in Chapter 5 for additional information.

8. Match the spread with the option strike image and identify a strategy example for A and B.

   A. Horizontal spread—2. Call calendar spread, put calendar spread.

   B. Vertical spread—1. Bull call spread, bear call spread, bear put spread, bull put spread.

   C. Diagonal spread—3.

9. Assuming a call calendar spread has reached the first expiration month and the short call has expired worthless, and given a bullish outlook for the security, the strategist can (a) hold the remaining long call to sell it at an opportune time, or (b) _____ to create a bull call spread.

    Answer: A—Sell another higher-strike call.

    Discussion: A bull call spread consists of a long lower-strike-price call and a short higher-strike call with the same expiration dates. The maximum reward is achieved when the stock trades at or above the higher strike price (moves upward) and the strategy used is consistent with a bullish outlook.

10. True or false: A bull call spread is a debit spread created by purchasing a lower-strike call and simultaneously selling a higher-strike call on the same underlying with the same expiration date.

    Answer: True.

    Discussion: This is the definition of a bull call spread.

11. _____ is a type of form required for a customer wishing to add options trading to a brokerage account.

    Answer: C—Option Approval Form.

    Discussion: Brokerages are required to obtain specific information from prospective option traders prior to granting access to such instruments. The purpose is to determine suitability of such trading based on experience and financial health. The types of strategies in which an individual is eligible to trade depend on the option approval level granted based on the information provided.

12. True or false: The more complicated the strategy, the lower the option approval required.

    Answer: False.

    Discussion: Most brokerages have option approval levels from 0 to 4 or from 1 to 5, the higher levels being associated with more complex strategies with greater risk.

13. True or false: In the event a trader does not have access to option analysis software, it is acceptable for the trader to enter a trade without calculating the risk and reward.

Answer: False.

Discussion: A trader must always understand and quantify the risk associated with strategies used and positions created. This information should be calculated by hand, if needed.

MEDIA ASSIGNMENT

This media assignment requires you to make an intermediate market assessment for the NASDAQ 100 Index Trust (QQQQ) using whatever form of analysis you prefer (fundamental, technical, or sentiment). This can be accomplished by using the newspaper, journals, or other print media (providing it's your outlook). Once again we will use the Internet to complete our analysis and will complete this exercise using a simple technical technique.

The Optionetics web site has free access to fundamental data, technical charts, option chains, and detailed quotes. Simply enter www.optionetics.com into the web browser and you'll be on your way. A daily chart for the QQQQ is displayed after entering the symbol in the "quotes/options" field and selecting "Chart" in the drop-down menu immediately to the right of this field (see Figure 5.1). Once the chart appears, a couple of indicators are added and the chart size is adjusted as follows:

- Add a 50-day (lighter, longer line) and 200-day MA (darker, shorter line).
- Change chart size to "Large."
- Select "Update Chart."

The 50-day MA represents roughly 2.5 months of trading and falls nicely in our outlook period. This particular number was selected because it is a commonly viewed MA—a 40-day MA is the outlook midpoint, but less widely followed. The 200-day MA is added to gain a sense of the more dominant longer-term trend. It appears that price is pulling back slightly after a strong upward trend that began in November 2005. However, both the intermediate trend and long-term trend are bullish, as seen by the upward-trending MAs. Diminishing volume on the pullback appears to confirm continued upward movement on an intermediate basis.

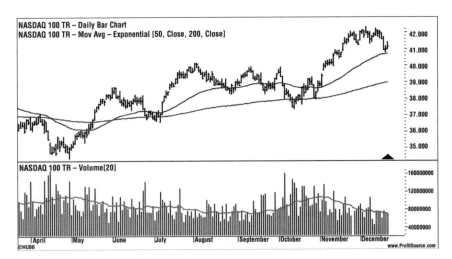

FIGURE 5.1 Daily Chart for QQQQ with Moving Averages and Volume (*Source:* www.ProfitSource.com)

Given this bullish outlook, we opt to evaluate a bull call spread. Although we are potentially limiting our reward compared to a single long call position, we are also minimizing risk by reducing the total value of the position. Moving to the top of this web page, we now select "Option Chain" from the drop-down menu and note that a long list of call options is available (see Figure 5.2).

A bull call spread using the QQQQ February 41 call as the lower long leg of the spread and the QQQQ February 43 call as the higher short leg of the spread results in a debit of $0.85 per spread ($1.10 − $0.25). If the ETF moves to $43 or higher by February expiration, the position can be closed for a credit of $2, yielding a $1.15 profit. This is compared to a straight call position with a cost of $1.10 and unlimited profit potential. Assuming a move to exactly $43, the long call would yield a $1.90 profit.

The risk/reward ratio for the bull call spread is 1.15 to 0.85, or 1.35 to 1. Not exactly a stellar scenario, but the strategy is valid for the security outlook. It is up to the individual trader to determine if the limited risk position is worthwhile.

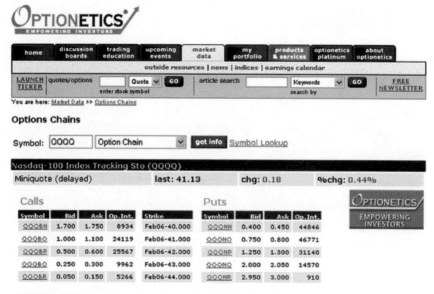

FIGURE 5.2   Partial Option Chain for QQQQ (*Source:* www.Optionetics.com)

VOCABULARY DEFINITIONS

Bear put spread: A vertical put spread that creates a debit in the account and is established by purchasing a higher-strike put and selling a lower-strike put with the same expiration dates. The bear put strategy has both limited profit potential and limited downside risk.

Bull call spread: A vertical call spread that creates a debit in the account and is established by purchasing a lower-strike call and selling a higher-strike call with the same expiration dates. The bull call strategy has both limited profit potential and limited downside risk.

Calendar spread: The calendar spread is a strategy that can be used when a gradual trend or sideways move in the underlying security is expected. It is sometimes called a *horizontal spread* or *time spread* because it uses two options with the same strike price but different expiration dates. In most cases, the option strategist creates a calendar spread by purchasing a longer-term option and selling a short-term option.

Collar spread: A protective put position with costs that are offset by adding a short call for the underlying stock. It generally is constructed using one long put and one short call for every 100 shares of stock and is used when the strategist is short-term bearish to neutral on the stock, but longer-term bullish.

Compliance department: A group within a brokerage firm that monitors the company's activities and the activities of its registered representatives to determine whether they are complying with securities laws and regulations, and to alert those responsible when such conditions are not met. This group participates in the option approval process for accounts.

Diagonal spread: A combination of a vertical and a horizontal spread, which can include different expiration dates and different strike prices. For example, buying a longer-term call option and selling a shorter-term call option with a higher strike price is an example of a diagonal spread.

Horizontal spread: Another term used to describe a calendar spread. The horizontal spread uses two options with the same strike prices and different expiration dates. This type of spread can be created with puts or calls.

Naked call: A short call option position that is not protected by existing shares of stock for the underlying. In the event the call writer is assigned (called out of the underlying), he or she will be short shares and must cover the position by purchasing the underlying in the market. This is an unlimited-risk, limited-reward position and is not recommended.

Protective put: A position that combines long stock and a long put, with the put serving as downside protection for the stock position. It generally is constructed using one put for every 100 shares of stock and is used when the strategist is short-term bearish on the stock, but longer-term bullish.

Rolling: A term used to describe a position adjustment where the strategist switches an existing option (closes a position) with a longer-term option (opens a position) for the same underlying. When the option is rolled up, the new position uses a higher strike price, and when it is rolled down, the new position uses a lower strike price.

Stop-loss: A price level that triggers an alert or trade in order to minimize losses in a new position or prevent losses in a position that has unrealized gains. When a trader is long a position the stop-loss is below the current market for the security, and when short a position the stop-loss is above the current market.

Trading level: The trading level is the option strategy approval for the account, as dictated by the brokerage firm's compliance group. Factors impacting the option trading level include the account type, the experience of all account holders, and the financial standing of all account holders.

Vertical spread: A trade that involves the simultaneous purchase and sale of options on the same stock with the same expiration date. The only difference between the options that are purchased and those that are sold is the strike price. Vertical spreads get their name from the image they create using an option table and can be created with puts or calls.

CHAPTER 6

Basic Strategies Using Put Options

SUMMARY

In this chapter, we add basic and combination option strategies centered around put positions. Recall, a put option gives the owner the right, but not the obligation, to sell the underlying stock at a specific price until the expiration date. The owner can "put" the stock to the option writer. The value of the put option contract will increase as the price of the underlying asset falls. Once again, quite a few trade strategies were discussed, so it is helpful to summarize them here in Table 6.1.

It is important to reiterate that although a strategy may satisfy a given outlook, it is also possible that a different strategy may be more suitable for the current conditions or risk/reward potential. The relative volatility level is one such condition that merits attention. Selling premium in a low-volatility environment may make it difficult to obtain the risk/reward ratio you seek. In addition, the strike prices and expiration months selected when implementing an option strategy have a large impact on the ultimate risk of the position. In a put calendar spread, if the trader opts to establish a position that uses the short put as the leg with a longer term to expiration, the risk is similar to a naked short put, regardless of the price of the underlying.

TABLE 6.1 Put Strategy Matrix

Strategy	Position	Market Conditions	Risk/ Reward	Acceptable
Long put	Long put	Bearish	Limited/ limited (high)	Yes
Short put	Short put	Bullish, neutral	Limited (high)/ limited	No
Bear put spread	Long higher strike, short lower strike (1:1)	Bearish	Limited/ limited	Yes
Bull put spread	Long lower strike, short higher strike (1:1)	Bullish, neutral	Limited/ limited	Yes*
Put calendar spread	Long longer term, short shorter term (1:1)	Neutral to bearish	Limited/ limited	Yes
Protective put	Long stock, long put (100 shares per 1 put)	Short-term bearish, long-term bullish	Limited/ unlimited	Yes
Covered put	Short stock, short put (100 shares per 1 put)	Short-term neutral, long-term bearish	Unlimited/ limited	No

*The strategy has risk that is limited and is therefore acceptable; however, a different strategy may better serve the trader's outlook from a risk/reward scenario.

QUESTIONS AND EXERCISES

1. The value of the put option contract will _____ as the price of the underlying asset falls.

   A. Decrease.

   B. Remain neutral.

   C. Increase.

   D. Expire.

2. Combination trades can include the following securities:
   A. Shares of stock, puts, and/or calls.
   B. Shares of stock and the underlying index.
   C. Calls and the underlying index.
   D. None of the above.

3. Since the final weeks of an option's life represent a period of accelerating time decay, it is generally recommended that _____ be closed 30 days prior to expiration.
   A. Long positions in a spread.
   B. Short positions in a spread.
   C. Single long positions.
   D. Single short positions.

4. True or false: The maximum profit occurs for a long put when the price of the underlying falls to zero.

5. True or false: A protective put is another name for a married put.

6. The _____ is an option position with the contract obligation guaranteed by liquid assets deposited into the account.
   A. Protected put.
   B. Cash-secured put.
   C. Married put.
   D. Short put.

7. Match the strategy with the security outlook.
   A. Bull put spread   _____ 1. Bearish.
   B. Bear put spread   _____ 2. Generally neutral, then bearish.
   C. Bear call spread   _____ 3. Bearish to neutral.
   D. Put calendar spread _____ 4. Bullish to neutral.

8. True or false: *Pin risk* is the term used to define risk associated with a short option position when the underlying asset closes very near the strike price at expiration.

9. The short shares in a covered put position are completely protected by the _____.
   A. Short put.
   B. Long put.
   C. Short call.
   D. None of the above.

10. True or false: Since a covered put includes stock, the position risk and margin requirements are both very low.

11. A put calendar spread with a longer-term long put option and a shorter-term short put option is beneficial when the strategist's outlook is _____.
   A. Neutral to bearish.
   B. Wrong.
   C. Bearish, then bullish.
   D. Bullish.

12. A bear put spread reduces the risk of a long put by decreasing both the total investment and the impact of _____ on the total premium.
   A. Volatility.
   B. Time decay.
   C. Recessions.
   D. Market makers' profits.

13. True or false: Trading on margin is sometimes referred to as a double-edged sword since the impact of leverage amplifies both profits and losses.

MEDIA ASSIGNMENT

At this point we have examined option strategies that can be used for a variety of market conditions. It is not uncommon to get comfortable with one or two strategies and forget about others that could potentially enhance your trading. This media assignment requires the construction of a paper trade using a strategy from the ones described in Chapter 5 or 6 that you find least intuitive. The research needed to complete this assignment is most efficient via the Internet, so if you can gain access to the web via your library, it will be helpful.

Review the conditions that are optimal for the selected strategies, then analyze various broad market and sector indexes using your preferred method of analysis. Identify an index that fits the conditions needed for your strategy. Next, using information from the earlier chapters in *The Index Trading Course*, identify an ETF that tracks the performance of the particular sector. Ideally the ETF will also have options traded on it—a fast way to determine this is to enter the ETF symbol in the Optionetics Quote area and select "Chain" from the drop-down menu. As seen in other assignments, a comprehensive option chain will be displayed if one exists (see Figure 6.1).

If it is difficult to find an ETF with options that fits your strategy, go to a web site that provides information about the components of the base index or the top holdings of the ETF (your broker's web site may contain such data) and review those stocks; chances are options will trade on those individual securities. This creates an extra step because you will then have to analyze the individual stock to confirm that the conditions (bullish/bearish, high volatility/low volatility) are similar to the original

FIGURE 6.1 Determining Whether an ETF Has an Option Chain (*Source:* www .Optionetics.com)

analysis you completed. Also, it deviates from the primary goal of this text, namely index-based trading.

Once your analysis is completed and you've identified the strategy and security, you will construct the paper trade by writing out the underlying security, symbol, and last price, as well as the options used for the trade, including the strike prices and expiration dates. Also identify whether the specific option will be held long or short, and the last bid or offer for the option, depending on whether you will be buying or selling it. You can enter this information on a software spreadsheet if you wish.

In the next chapter we will identify the risk, reward, and breakevens for this trade, create a risk graph, and establish guidelines to monitor the performance of the paper trade.

VOCABULARY LIST

Bear put spread	Hedge
Bull put spread	Margin
Cash-secured put	Married put
Covered put	Pin risk
Execute	Protective put
Fill	Rolling

SOLUTIONS

1. The value of the put option contract will _____ as the price of the underlying asset falls.

   Answer: C—Increase.

   Discussion: A put gives the holder the right to sell the underlying at a set price, by a set date. This right becomes more valuable as the price of the underlying declines. Long put holders are bearish while short put holders are bullish.

2. Combination trades can include the following securities:

   Answer: A—Shares of stock, puts, and/or calls.

   Discussion: Trades can include simply puts or calls (long only or spreads); a combination of the two (straddle—described in the next chapter); stock and puts (protective put); stock and calls (covered call); or stock, puts, and calls (collar). Recall that a trader cannot own an index; for this reason options for equity indexes are cash settled.

3. Since the final weeks of an option's life represent a period of accelerating time decay, it is generally recommended that _____ be closed 30 days prior to expiration.

   Answer: C—Single long positions.

   Discussion: By selling the long portion of a spread, the option strategist is left with a short put or call. These positions represent unlimited risk and limited but high risk, respectively, and are not recommended. Even on the last day of trading, a strategist will be subject to pin risk on the short contract if the long side is closed. A strong, unusual move in the underlying in the last few hours of trading could completely negate the reason for entering the spread in the first place—to limit risk. Therefore, it is recommended that single long positions be closed 30 days prior to expiration, but not necessarily the long portion of a combination position.

4. True or false: The maximum profit occurs for a long put when the underlying price falls to zero.

   Answer: True.

   Discussion: When a stock trade approaches zero, the trader will have a profit equal to the strike price minus the current price of the underlying (equal to zero) minus the original cost of the put. While the profit potential is not unlimited, it is high.

5. True or false: A protective put is another name for a married put.

   Answer: False.

   Discussion: Although a protective put and a married put consist of the same securities, a married put is a specific type of protective put position. In a married put, the underlying shares and option position are purchased at the same time, while a put can be added to an already existing position to create a protective put.

6. The _____ is an option position with the contract obligation guaranteed by liquid assets deposited into the account.

   Answer: B—Cash-secured put.

   Discussion: A cash-secured put is a short put position that is protected by a sufficient amount of cash deposited into the account to meet the writer's obligation. The cash remains available in the account throughout the life of the short put.

7. Match the strategy with the security outlook.

   Answer:

   A. Bull put spread—4. Bullish to neutral.

   B. Bear put spread—1. Bearish.

   C. Bear call spread—3. Bearish to neutral.

   D. Put calendar spread—2. Generally neutral, then bearish.

8. True or false: *Pin risk* is the term used to define risk associated with a short option position when the underlying asset closes very near the strike price at expiration.

   Answer: True.

   Discussion: Different brokerages have different cut-off times to provide exercise instructions for expiring options. This cut-off is generally within one to a few hours after the close for retail customers. As a result, news hitting the markets after the close exacerbates this pin risk, which may prompt long option holders to exercise their rights even when the underlying closes slightly below the strike price (for calls). An individual who holds a spread with the short leg subjected to pin risk needs to monitor the situation and manage his or her risk into the expiration weekend.

9. The short shares in a covered put position are completely protected by the _____.

   Answer: D—None of the above.

   Discussion: Since a short put represents an obligation rather than a right, the short put holder has no control over being assigned on a particular put. A strong move upward diminishes the likelihood of assignment on the short put, while creating losses for the short stock position. Since a stock can technically move upward indefinitely, such a position represents unlimited risk.

10. True or false: Since a covered put includes stock, the position risk and margin requirements are both very low.

    Answer: False.

    Discussion: A covered put includes a short stock position with unlimited risk. As a result, the minimum requirements include 150 percent margin, similar to any other short stock position. In order to best understand the risk and requirement for various combination positions, consider what the ramifications are when the price of the underlying moves to different levels (i.e., below the short sale price, above the short put strike price, etc.).

11. A put calendar spread with a longer-term long put option and a shorter-term short put option is beneficial when the strategist's outlook is _____.

    Answer: A—Neutral to bearish.

    Discussion: The put calendar spread includes a long-term put and short-term put with the same strike price, but different expiration dates. Neutral or sideways price action that occurs prior to expiration of the short put will result in the short put losing value more quickly than the long, further out put (due to accelerated time decay into expiration). This is ideal since the short side was sold for a credit. Assuming the short-term put expires worthless, the trader will then have a long put remaining, which benefits when the price of the underlying moves downward. Neutral to moderately bullish conditions followed by bearish conditions are optimal for the put calendar spread described here.

12. A bear put spread reduces the risk of a long put by decreasing both the total investment and the impact of _____ on the total premium.

    Answer: B—Time decay.

    Discussion: Time is the second most important factor in an option's price. Although time decay has a negative impact for a long contract holder, it is positive and desirable for the short contract holder. Since a bear put spread combines the two positions, it reduces the total impact of time decay for the trader.

13. True or false: Trading on margin is sometimes referred to as a double-edged sword since the impact of leverage amplifies both profits and losses.

Answer: True.

Discussion: Novice traders can get caught up in the excitement of double-digit performance when they are leveraged and begin trading on the right side of the market. A $5,000 margin purchase of $10,000 worth of securities has a 20 percent return when the position moves up $1,000. However, the same holds true for a $1,000 move downward. Losses are not split between the trader and the brokerage firm lending the funds—the entire loss is borne by the trader.

MEDIA ASSIGNMENT

This media assignment prompted the reader to construct a paper trade using a strategy from Chapter 5 or 6 that was less intuitive than the others. Although the current (late 2005) low-volatility environment makes calendar spreads slightly more challenging, this strategy was selected because there will be a follow-up exercise on this assignment in the next chapter. A review of the broad market indexes suggests the markets may be consolidating or pulling back slightly after a nice strong upward move into year end. Such an outlook (short-term bearish to neutral, longer-term bullish) is consistent with a call calendar spread strategy.

The review included an assessment of weekly and daily charts using moving averages (20-day and 50-day), trendlines, and volume. During a sector review, it was noted that the NASDAQ Biotechnology Index ($NBI) is displaying similar characteristics (short-term bearish to neutral, longer-term bullish); however, it is also running into resistance put in place in late 2003 and early 2004. If the index can move past this resistance on the next push, a nice upward move may ensue. The iShares Biotechnology Index (IBB) tracks this biotech index and will be used to construct a trade (go to www.ishares.com and bring up Sector ETFs to locate one source of sector-based ETFs).

A check to confirm options are available for this ETF was completed by accessing the Optionetics web site (www.optionetics.com) and entering the symbol in the Quote area, then requesting an option chain (as described in the Media Assignment section). Options are available for this ETF, and the chain provided will be used as a basis for constructing the trade. If options were not available, a check of the ETF on the AMEX web

TABLE 6.2 Analyzing the Spread

Call Calendar Spread	Symbol	Recent Price	Long/Short	Cost of Spread
iShares Biotech	IBB	78.18		
January 80 Call	IBBAP	0.85	Ask (short)	−0.85
March 80 Call	IBBCP	2.70	Bid (long)	+2.70
				+1.85

site (www.amex.com) allows us to bring up top holdings for the ETF. This is also available at the iShares web site, as well as other web sites.

Assuming 80 will serve as short-term resistance for IBB, a call calendar spread with an 80 strike price will be constructed. In order to give the position time to push past this potentially significant resistance area, a March 80 call will be considered as the long leg for the trade. The option chain was used to get quotes for these calls (see Table 6.2) and analyze the spread.

The initial debit to create the calendar spread on the IBB ETF is $1.85.

VOCABULARY DEFINITIONS

Bear put spread: A vertical put spread that creates a debit in the account and is established by purchasing a higher-strike put and selling a lower-strike put with the same expiration date. The bear put strategy has both limited profit potential and limited downside risk.

Bull put spread: A vertical credit spread that is composed of buying a lower-strike put and selling a higher-strike put with the same expiration date. The bull put strategy has both limited profit potential and limited downside risk.

Cash-secured put: A cash-secured put is a short put position that is protected by a sufficient amount of cash deposited into the account to meet the writer's obligation. The cash remains available in the account throughout the life of the short put.

Covered put: A covered put is a position that combines short stock with a short put. In the event the underlying moves upward past the put strike price, the trader is left with an expired option and a short stock position. This is a strategy with unlimited risk.

Execute: Execute refers to the completion of a trade—a brokerage executes a buy order on your behalf.

Fill: An order that is placed and executed (completed) is said to be filled. Generally the details of the execution are also included (price and time). Combination orders that are placed specifically as such will only be filled for complete combinations; the trader will not have the short portion of a bear put spread executed without the long leg also being filled.

Hedge: A position that is established to minimize or completely eliminate risk due to an existing investment. In option trading, adjustments to a hedge may be necessary to maintain the intended protection.

Margin: Amounts deposited into an account when an investor borrows money from a broker for the purpose of establishing a securities position are referred to as margin. The margin required for specific positions varies, but is a minimum of 50 percent for long stock purchases. The margin requirement for a short position is minimally 150 percent—100 percent is deposited in the account from the sale of the security, and a minimum of 50 percent is deposited by the account holder. Short option positions have margin calculations that are partially based on the margin requirements of the underlying security and partially based on the protection provided by a second option on the underlying, as appropriate.

Married put: The position created when long stock is purchased at the same time as a long put. The put is used to hedge or protect the long shares, with the intention of exercising the put if needed. A married put position can be classified as a covered put; however, the reverse is not true. Not all covered puts are married puts.

Pin risk: A risk an option writer faces when the price of the underlying asset closes at or very near the strike price of the option. It is an important factor in selling options because if the asset closes at or very near the strike price upon expiration, the option holder might exercise the option and the writer will be faced with assignment.

Protective put: A position that combines long stock and a long put, with the put serving as downside protection for the stock position. It generally is constructed using one put for every 100 shares of stock and is used when the strategist is short-term bearish on the stock, but longer-term bullish.

Rolling: A term used to describe a position adjustment where the strategist switches an existing option (closes a position) with a longer-term option (opens a position) for the same underlying. When the option is rolled up, the new position uses a higher strike price, and when it is rolled down, the new position uses a lower strike price.

CHAPTER 7

Complex and Advanced Strategies

SUMMARY

In this final option-specific chapter, the trader is introduced to more complex strategies. Although a variety of these are discussed, they are not all recommended. As always, those strategies with unlimited or limited but high risk are not recommended. Why take such risk if there are alternate strategies that are consistent with the strategist's outlook? Table 7.1 shows a review of most of the strategies discussed.

Once an appropriate strategy is identified, the trader needs to determine if the risk/reward ratio is acceptable. While complex strategies make the assessment a touch more complicated, it is still quite manageable. The markets are consistently providing option traders with opportunities to make money, so don't rush into a trade that doesn't maximize your return.

TABLE 7.1   Advanced Strategy Matrix

Strategy	Position	Market Conditions	Risk/ Reward	Acceptable
Long straddle	Long call, long put	Strong move pending	Limited/ unlimited	Yes
Long strangle	Long higher-strike call, long lower-strike put	Strong move pending	Limited/ unlimited	Yes
Short straddle	Short call, short put	Neutral	Unlimited/ limited	No
Short strangle	Short higher-strike call, short lower-strike put	Neutral	Unlimited/ limited	No
Ratio backspread	Long option, short option (2:1, 3:2)	Directional bias	Limited/ limited (high)	Yes
Butterfly	Bull spread plus bear spread (same option type)	Neutral (range-bound)	Limited/ limited	Yes
Iron butterfly	Bull spread plus bear spread (different option type)	Neutral (range-bound)	Limited/ limited	Yes
Diagonal spread	Longer-term long option, shorter-term short option	Neutral, then directional bias	Limited/ limited	Yes

QUESTIONS AND EXERCISES

1. The long straddle has significant _____ associated with it, so the move expected must be substantial to benefit the trader.

   A. Time decay.

   B. Premium.

   C. Risk.

   D. Delta.

2. A second strategy—similar to the long straddle—that relies on a strong move in the underlying is the _____.
   A. Short straddle.
   B. Long strangle.
   C. Short strangle.
   D. Long lasso.

3. The Greek used to measure the change in the option premium relative to the change in the underlying is _____.
   A. Alpha.
   B. Vega.
   C. Delta.
   D. Theta.

4. True or false: A long straddle or strangle with a net positive delta has an upward directional bias.

5. The long butterfly is a popular strategy to employ when traders expect the stock or market to trade _____.
   A. Unpredictably.
   B. Directionally.
   C. Predictably.
   D. Within a range.

6. The iron butterfly combines a _____ spread and a _____ spread.
   A. Bull / bear.
   B. Caterpillar / deer.
   C. Bull / bull.
   D. Lion / tiger.

7. One more go at it—match the strategy with the security outlook.
   A. Call iron butterfly   _____   1. Explosively directional.
   B. Put ratio spread   _____   2. Neutral, then longer-term bullish.
   C. Long strangle   _____   3. Bearish.
   D. Call diagonal spread   _____   4. Range-bound.

8. True or false: The collar includes stock, puts, and calls and is a strategy used to protect a position.

9. True or false: A diagonal spread is similar to a calendar spread, but the options in a diagonal spread have the same strike price.

10. In order to determine the net delta of a long straddle, the delta of the call is _____ the delta of the put.
    A. Added to.
    B. Subtracted from.
    C. Multiplied by.
    D. Divided by.

11. In order to determine the net delta of a short straddle, the delta of the call is _____ the delta of the put.
    A. Added to.
    B. Subtracted from.
    C. Multiplied by.
    D. Divided by.

MEDIA ASSIGNMENT

The assignment for this section follows up on some work completed for Chapter 6. Locate the trade you constructed previously so you can evaluate the risk, reward, and breakevens for the combination position. We will also establish some guidelines for monitoring the position going forward. Table 7.2, a call calendar spread, was created in the assignment for Chapter 6.

TABLE 7.2 Call Calendar Spread Analysis

Call Calendar Spread	Symbol	Recent Price	Long/Short	Cost of Spread
iShares Biotech	IBB	78.18		
January 80 Call	IBBAP	0.85	Ask (short)	−0.85
March 80 Call	IBBCP	2.70	Bid (long)	+2.70
				+1.85

The initial debit to create the calendar spread on the IBB ETF is $1.85.

Create a spreadsheet, using graph paper or a computer, that will allow you to monitor the following information:

- The price for the underlying.
- The ask for the short call and the bid for the long call.
- Position value.
- The delta for both calls.
- The theta for both calls.

The goal for this assignment is to observe the change in value for the options, based on changes in the underlying ETF and delta, as well as the impact of time decay. Review all of these factors preferably two to three times per week for four weeks, or at minimum once a week. Greeks are available from a variety of web sites including the Philadelphia Stock Exchange's web site (www.phlx.com). Access the "Quotes & Trade Info" section on the left side of the home page, enter the symbol needed, and select "Options" from the drop-down menu. Optionetics Platinum also provides extensive options data, including the Greeks.

If you do not have regular access to the Internet, locate a high-volume index or ETF with options quoted in a business newspaper. Create a trade that can be monitored by minimally noting the price at closing of the underlying and the closing price of the options (must be liquid for closing price to be near the closing bid-ask for the option). Try to obtain delta and theta values a couple of times during the life of the position by accessing a computer at the library.

When creating a paper trade, it's nice to note the end result and either be thankful your money wasn't on the line or feel positive because you felt comfortable with the strategy. Since so many things impact option combination price, it's really important to observe what is happening throughout the life of the option when completing a paper trade. Although it is not the same as having your money on the line, it is helpful.

VOCABULARY LIST

Butterfly	Ratio backspread
Delta	Ratio spread
Delta neutral	Straddle
Directional bias	Strangle
Gamma	Theta
Iron butterfly	Vega
Pin risk	

SOLUTIONS

1. The long straddle has significant _____ associated with it, so the move expected must be substantial to benefit the trader.

   Answer: B—Premium.

   Discussion: Since this combination position includes the purchase of two options, the initial investment is relatively higher than with other option combinations. As a result, the price move required for the underlying is significant to reach the breakeven.

2. A second strategy—similar to the long straddle—that relies on a strong move in the underlying is the _____.

   Answer: B—Long strangle.

   Discussion: A long strangle is similar to a long straddle in that they both have a long call and a long put that expire in the same month. The long straddle's options use the same at-the-money strike price while the long strangle uses different out-of-the-money strike prices for the put and call.

3. The Greek used to measure the change in the option premium relative to the change in the underlying is _____.

   Answer: C—Delta.

   Discussion: Delta is defined as the change in the price of an option relative to the change of the underlying security. One share of long stock has a fixed delta of +1 (bullish), while one share of short stock has a fixed delta of –1 (bearish). Options, in contrast, have variable deltas, with call option deltas positive (between 0 and 1) and put option deltas negative (between 0 and –1). Stocks and options can be combined to create a delta neutral position that is minimally impacted by changes in the underlying asset. However, since option deltas are variable, changes in the underlying asset eventually impact the position, resulting in one that is net bullish (positive delta) or net bearish (negative delta).

4. True or false: A long straddle or strangle with a net positive delta has an upward directional bias.

Answer: True.

Discussion: Call options (bullish) have positive deltas while put options (bearish) have negative deltas. As the price of a stock moves upward, we expect the price of a call associated with this stock to move upward while the puts move downward—thus the negative delta. A combination position is designated a delta value by adding the component deltas together. The net positive delta suggests that a long straddle or strangle has a bullish bias since the delta of the call is greater than the delta of the put on an absolute basis.

5. The long butterfly is a popular strategy to employ when traders expect the stock or market to trade _____.

Answer: D—Within a range.

Discussion: The long butterfly combines a bullish spread with a bearish spread. Since these two types of spreads are moving in counter directions, the optimal situation for the combined position is one that is range-bound.

6. The iron butterfly combines a _____ spread and a _____ spread.

Answer: A—Bull / bear.

Discussion: The iron butterfly is a combination strategy that includes both puts and calls with four different options contracts. It can be viewed as a combination of a bear call spread that consists of a short at-the-money call and a long out-of-the money call, along with a bull put spread that consists of a long out-of-the-money put with a short at-the-money put.

7. Match the term with its definition by placing the proper number in the space provided.

   Answer:

   A. Call iron butterfly—4. Range-bound.

   B. Put ratio spread—3. Bearish.

   C. Long strangle—1. Explosively directional.

   D. Call diagonal spread—2. Neutral, then longer-term bullish.

8. True or false: The collar includes stock, puts, and calls and is a strategy used to protect a position.

   Answer: True.

   Discussion: The collar is a covered call and a protective put (which involves the purchase of shares and puts) wrapped into one. The idea is to gain downside protection from the put, but to offset the cost of this protection with the sale of a call. This strategy is generally implemented when the trader is moderately bullish or neutral on a stock, but wants protection in case of a bearish move to the downside.

9. True or false: A diagonal spread is similar to a calendar spread, but the options in a diagonal spread have the same strike price.

   Answer: False.

   Discussion: The calendar spread uses the same strike price for the two options used to construct it. It is sometimes called a horizontal spread or time spread because it uses two options with the same strike price but different expiration dates. In most cases, the option strategist creates a calendar spread by purchasing a longer-term option and selling a short-term option. The diagonal spread generally makes use of different strike prices (for a visual depiction, see the charts under question 8 in Chapter 5 of this workbook).

10. In order to determine the net delta of a long straddle, the delta of the call is _____ the delta of the put.

    Answer: A—Added to.

    Discussion: A combination position is designated a delta value by adding the component deltas together. Recall that long call deltas are positive and long put deltas are negative.

11. In order to determine the net delta of a short straddle the delta of the call is _____ the delta of the put.

    Answer: A—Added to.

    Discussion: A combination position is designated a delta value by adding the component deltas together, regardless of whether the position is long or short. The trader is impacted by movement in the underlying based on whether the position was traded long or short, but the position itself will move upward or downward based on the underlying stock and the position's delta.

MEDIA ASSIGNMENT

This media assignment required the reader to determine the risk, reward, and breakevens for the position created in the previous assignment and to monitor price changes. The monitoring will be completed using a spreadsheet that tracks the following information:

- The price for the underlying.
- The ask for the short call and the bid for the long call.
- Position value.
- The delta for both calls.
- The theta for both calls.

The risk for the trade is calculated by starting with the risk from the short option, in this case the January 80 call. By itself, this position represents an unlimited risk position. If the stock moves above 80 and the trader is assigned, he would hold a short stock position that could technically rise indefinitely. However, in our example, the long option is held at the same strike price and can be used in the event of assignment on the short call. There are actually a couple of choices for the trader in the event this occurs, but this will be used in our example. Since the short stock would be covered through exercise at the same strike price, the risk for the position is the initial debit amount of $1.85, or $185 per calendar.

The reward associated with the combination is more complicated since there are two different expiration dates that can result in two substantially different reward scenarios. The best-case scenario includes a situation where IBB remains below 80 through January expiration, thus having the short option expire worthless. At that point, the trader is long a call option that has less value than when initially purchased, but has unlimited reward potential.

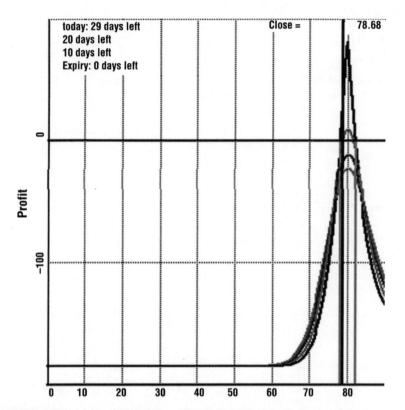

today: 29 days left
20 days left
10 days left
Expiry: 0 days left

Close =   78.68

FIGURE 7.1 Risk Graph for IBB Call Calendar Spread (*Source:* www
.Optionetics.com)

This is where the breakevens and costs become difficult to calculate for
a calendar spread. In order to determine the profit potential of the combined position at January expiration, we have to make assumptions about
the value of the long March option—with approximately two months to expiration. Figure 7.1 estimates these values using $78.22 as a downside
breakeven and $82.14 as an upside breakeven at January expiration. Using
the strike price of 80, the downside breakeven is approximately $1.78 below
the strike and the upside breakeven is approximately $2.14 above the strike,
reflecting increased value for the long call as IBB moves higher.

Although the risk/reward profile is pretty unappealing, we will continue
to monitor the trade to gain a better feel for the dynamics of the position at
January expiration. Figure 7.2 displays the data that will be monitored.

An initial decline in the value for the position reflects an issue en-

	12/22	12/23	12/27	12/29	12/30	1/3	1/5	1/9
IBB	78.18	78.99	78.01	77.54	77.24	78.40	79.73	81.84
IBBAP	−0.85	−1.05	−0.90	−0.65	−0.55	−0.85	−1.10	−2.45
delta		0.47	0.342	0.284	0.254	0.355	0.490	0.739
theta		−0.025	−0.034	−0.031	−0.030	−0.037	−0.040	−0.053
IBBCP	2.70	2.80	2.45	2.20	2.05	2.50	2.95	4.00
delta		0.490	0.452	0.425	0.408	0.467	0.538	0.661
theta		−0.021	−0.022	−0.022	−0.022	−0.024	−0.024	−0.024
Value	1.85	1.75	1.55	1.55	1.50	1.65	1.85	1.55

FIGURE 7.2 Spreadsheet for Monitoring Position

countered by all traders—slippage. As soon as we enter a long position at the asking price, we are affected by the spread in the option quote, which is at least $0.05 to $0.10 for options. The first column in the spreadsheet in Figure 7.2 reflects the bid price for the short position and the ask for the long position, while the remaining quotes reflect the ask for the short position and the bid for the long position. For this reason, Greeks were not included in the first column.

VOCABULARY DEFINITIONS

Butterfly: A butterfly is a combination strategy that works well in range-bound markets and can be created with puts or calls. A call butterfly consists of a long in-the-money call, two short calls with a higher strike price, and another call with an even higher strike price. It can be thought of as a combination of a bull call spread and a bear call spread.

Delta: Change in the price of an option relative to the change in the underlying security.

Delta neutral: A position that is constructed in such a way that the net delta of all components is equal to zero—this position is relatively insensitive to the price movement of underlying instruments.

Directional bias: A trend outlook that is upward or downward. Directional bias also refers to a strategy characteristic—a strategy that has directional bias requires a bullish or bearish move.

Gamma: Change in the delta of an option with respect to the change in price of its underlying security.

Iron butterfly: The iron butterfly is a combination strategy used in range-bound markets that includes both puts and calls with four different options contracts. It can be viewed as a combination of a bear call spread consisting of a short at-the-money call and a long out-of-the-money call, along with a bull put spread that consists of a long out-of-the-money put with a short at-the-money put.

Pin risk: A risk an option writer faces when the price of the underlying asset closes at or very near the strike price of the option. It is an important factor in selling options because if the asset closes at or very near the strike price upon expiration, the options holder might exercise the option and the writer will be faced with assignment.

Ratio backspread: A ratio backspread is created by purchasing one side of the trade and selling another in a disproportionate ratio, but it is the opposite of the ratio spread. A ratio backspread is created by buying more options than one is selling.

Ratio spread: A ratio spread is created by buying one side of the trade and selling another in a disproportionate ratio. A ratio spread is created by selling more options than one is buying. This leaves the strategist with a naked position and is not recommended. Traders should focus instead on credit spreads, backspreads, and other lower-risk strategies when looking for opportunities to sell premium.

Straddle: A combination position that consists of a call and a put (1:1) with the same strike prices and expiration dates. The long straddle includes a long call and a long put and is a limited-risk, unlimited-reward position that requires an explosive move in either direction to be profitable. The short straddle has unlimited risk and is not recommended.

Strangle: A combination position that consists of a call and a put (1:1) with different strike prices and the same expiration date. The long strangle includes a long call and a long put and is a limited-risk, unlimited-reward position that requires an explosive move in either direction to be profitable. The short strangle has unlimited risk and is not recommended.

Theta: Change in the price of an option with respect to a change in its time to expiration (time value).

Vega: Change in the price of an option with respect to its change in volatility.

Catalysts

SUMMARY

Although a complete list of factors that impact the market is not available in any material we've ever seen, there is a handful that would likely appear on any such list that was attempted. We describe these factors as "catalysts" and focus our attention on them in Chapter 8. Recognize that the list is not all-inclusive and that they will carry different weights under different market conditions.

First, it's important to consider an important theory about the movement of stock prices. This theory, known as the Efficient Market Theory (EMT), postulates that the only thing that can effect a change in price is new information. Since the future and news are completely unpredictable, it follows that stock prices are erratic or random. As a result, those who subscribe to this market view believe that it is not possible to successfully trade the markets. By Chapter 8, you probably realize that we are not quite Efficient Market Theorists (a.k.a. "random walkers").

Regardless, EMT brought about a great product to which we certainly do subscribe—index mutual funds, and more importantly, exchange-traded funds (ETFs). These passively managed investment vehicles are the result of EMT's beliefs that you can't beat the markets and shouldn't really try (passive investing). ETFs offer index traders a great tool for their arsenals. Combined with option trading, these products provide a wide variety of profitable market conditions for individual traders.

What types of news affect the markets? As mentioned, if it was possible to develop such a list, it would likely be pretty long. Among top catalysts we include are monetary policy of the Federal Reserve; economic data that indicate inflation, growth, or a slowdown; certain commodity prices; and institutional trading activity.

QUESTIONS AND EXERCISES

1. Those who believe in the Efficient Market Theory _____ believe that you can successfully trade the markets.

    A. Do.

    B. Do not.

2. According to efficient market proponents, only _____ can move stock prices.

    A. Earnings.

    B. Analysts.

    C. New information.

    D. Automated systems.

3. Which type of fund is not actively managed and therefore has lower investor fees?

    A. Value fund.

    B. Index fund.

    C. No-load fund.

    D. Institutional fund.

4. True or false: Index funds seek to beat the markets.

5. _____ trade throughout the day like stocks.

    A. Index funds.

    B. Actively managed funds.

    C. Exchange-traded funds.

    D. Option funds.

6. True or false: Options trade on a variety of different ETFs.

7. Match the term with its definition by placing the proper number in the space provided. This particular exercise is geared toward call options.

   A. Fed funds rate _____ 1. Simultaneous purchase or sale of 15 or more stocks.

   B. Contagion _____ 2. Seeks to match the performance of the market.

   C. Discount rate _____ 3. The overnight rate the Fed charges member banks.

   D. Passive investing _____ 4. A global sell-off in the financial markets.

   E. Program trading _____ 5. The overnight rate member banks charge each other.

8. The NYSE _____ Index tracks the trades that represent upward movements versus trades that represent downward movements for stocks on the NYSE.

   A. Tick.
   B. Net Up.
   C. Change.
   D. Random.

9. Which report is not a key economic report?

   A. Monthly employment report.
   B. Consumer Price Index (CPI).
   C. Factory orders.
   D. Google earnings.

10. True or false: The simultaneous purchase or sale of 15 or more stocks worth less than $15 million is defined as program trading.

MEDIA ASSIGNMENT

There is one media assignment for this chapter that requires access to a business periodical (the business section of a daily newspaper may be sufficient) or a computer with Internet access. Any web site that provides news stories about economic reports and individual stocks—along with quotes—can be used. You will be making some observations about the impact news has on a specific stock.

Determine if there were any key economic reports released for the day being reported. Did these reports meet the market's expectations or were the numbers higher or lower than expected? How did the actual numbers impact the market, and how did market expectations play a role in this impact? If you need to obtain this information through a news article, be sure not to use the author's conclusions; draw your own, based on the data and market reaction only.

Next locate a stock with a news story for that day. How did the information from the story flow into the market? By the time a full article was written, it is likely that many market participants following that issue had already heard the news. Based on the type of news (bullish, bearish), to what extent was the stock move for the day consistent with this information?

Finally, if there was an important economic report or sector-specific news that involved the stock you're reviewing, what news played the most important role in the stock's movement for the day (or week)? Was price impacted more by general economic data or by company-specific information that was released?

VOCABULARY LIST

Buying pressure	Passive investing
Contagion	Portfolio insurance
Discount rate	Program trading
Downtick	Random walker
Efficient Market Theory	Retail investor
Federal Reserve	Selling pressure
Fed funds rate	Tick
Index fund	Uptick
Institutional investors	

SOLUTIONS

1. Those who believe in the Efficient Market Theory _____ believe that you can successfully trade the markets.

   Answer: B—Do not.

   Discussion: Efficient Market Theory holds that only new information can move stock prices. Since the future and news are completely unpredictable, it follows that stock prices are erratic or random. As a result, it isn't possible to successfully trade the market.

2. According to efficient market proponents, only _____ can move stock prices.

   Answer: C—New information.

   Discussion: The price of a stock is believed to be appropriate based on all of the information that all market participants hold about that stock. As a result, the only time that a price can change is when the information changes—that is, new information is introduced. The arrival of this new information is very quickly incorporated into the asset price.

3. Which type of fund is not actively managed and therefore has lower investor fees?

   Answer: B—Index fund.

   Discussion: A passively managed fund that seeks to match the performance of the index on which it is based is known as an index fund. These types of funds often outperform active funds and are a low-cost investment option.

4. True or false: Index funds seek to beat the markets.

   Answer: False.

   Discussion: Index funds seek to match the performance of the indexes on which they are based. They do not seek to outperform those indexes or the broad markets in general.

5. _____ trade throughout the day like stocks.

   Answer: C—Exchange-traded funds.

   Discussion: These passively managed investments can be traded throughout the day and are also eligible for short selling, providing the trader with a great deal of flexibility. Although these funds are also low-cost investments from the management fee perspective, costs associated with actively trading these instruments (commissions and slippage) can negate such a benefit.

6. True or false: Options trade on a variety of different ETFs.

   Answer: True.

   Discussion: An advantage to incorporating ETFs into a trading plan is that they provide traders with a variety of option strategies that can be used under many market conditions. Since ETFs and options can be traded long or short throughout the day, they are very flexible tools for the options strategist.

7. Match the term with its definition by placing the proper number in the space provided.

   Answer:

   A. Fed funds rate—5. The overnight rate member banks charge each other.

   B. Contagion—4. A global sell-off in the financial markets.

   C. Discount rate—3. The overnight rate the Fed charges member banks.

   D. Passive investing—2. Seeks to match the performance of the market.

   E. Program trading—1. Simultaneous purchase or sale of 15 or more stocks.

8. The NYSE _____ Index tracks the trades that represent upward movements versus trades that represent downward movements for stocks on the NYSE.

   Answer: A—Tick.

   Discussion: The term *tick* refers to the price change of an investment. It is defined as a movement in the price or quote of a security or contract. When a trade occurs at a higher price than the prior trade, the stock is on an uptick. Downticks occur when a stock's most recent trade occurs at a lower price than the prior trade. The NYSE Tick Index ($TICK) measures upticks minus downticks on the New York Stock Exchange at any given time.

9. Which report is not a key economic report?

   Answer: D—Google earnings.

   Discussion: Economic data is extremely important to index traders. Different reports take priority when the market has different concerns. Both the monthly employment report and CPI data rank high on a regular basis. Factory orders, while not as critical, still receive attention when released. Although various stock earnings reports may impact a security, a sector, or even the market, such reports do not fall under the heading of "economic report."

10. True or false: The simultaneous purchase or sale of 15 or more stocks worth less than $15 million is defined as program trading.

    Answer: False.

    Discussion: The simultaneous purchase or sale of 15 or more stocks worth *more than* $1 million is defined as program trading. Program trading is associated with the buying and selling by institutional investors and can move the markets.

MEDIA ASSIGNMENT

This media assignment is very media driven—we need to assess the impact of both economic data and stock-specific news on stock prices. Ideally you were able to evaluate a security that included both. If not, keep the exercise handy and pull it out on a more news-intensive day. Review the information with a discerning eye.

Although even business sections of a daily newspaper will include stock market information, generally market-focused publications such as the *Wall Street Journal* and *Investor's Business Daily* provide more complete coverage of both economic data releases and stock news. The wealth of information from financial web sites similarly provides more in-depth coverage even faster than these dailies. Since more isn't always better, be sure to focus your efforts on information you find most useful.

One source of market-moving information is the daily "Market Beat" article from the Optionetics web site. Other sources include MarketWatch, Yahoo! Finance, and your broker's web site. Assuming you are now proficient with surfing the Web, Figure 8.1 was retrieved from the Optionetics home page.

Optionetics Articles

Email this article to a friend

MARKET BEAT: Dec. 23

By Chris Tyler, Optionetics.com
12/23/2005 1:30 PM EST

EARLY TRADE

On the eve of the three-day Christmas break, the big guy in the in the suit looks to be somewhere far removed from Broad & Wall. While a couple a potential market-movers of note were released this morning, Wall Street has effectively put the brakes on, just as the Choo-Choo train finally started to leave the station. As of 11:10 ET, the NASDAQ Composite ($COMPQ) and S&P500 ($SPX) are registering a flat line result to a tepid, mouse-like -.10% decrease. With very holiday-inspired, but not-so-merry trading conditions, you could say that a lack of stirring is quite contagious ahead of the holiday.

One headline actually looked good on the surface, but was it really durable as far as a sustainable rally is concerned? The premarket release of the Durable Goods sounded strong as it came in with an increase of 4.4% and well-above analysts' estimates of 1.5%. However, while new orders came in at a record $223 billion, excluding the volatile transportation and aircraft components, core orders actually fell .6% for a third straight monthly decrease.

The other potential, scheduled catalyst in Friday's lethargy was the release of New Home Sales. Today's 11.3% plunge for the November period comes on the heels of a record surge witnessed in October. While the decrease was expected, the seasonally adjusted figure of 1.245 million units did fall shy of estimates calling for 1.310 million, with inventories rising 3.3% to a record 503,000 units and the largest glut in nine years.

FIGURE 8.1 Market Beat Clip from December 23, 2005 (*Source:* www .Optionetics.com)

Two notable pieces of economic data released on this particular day were the Durable Goods report and the New Home Sales data. While the first report included data that was mostly positive for the economy and generally positive for the markets, the second piece was more bearish for the consumer. Interestingly, both exceeded analysts' expectations, one on the upside and one on the downside. A market close that is modestly upward could reflect the bullish impact of the positive Durable Goods order, the less than stellar performance of the core data for that report, or a market snoozing the day before a three-day close. The other possibility is that the negative consumer report (New Home Sales) is putting a damper on the positive industrial report shown in Figure 8.2.

FIGURE 8.2 Market Data from December 23, 2005 (*Source:* Optionetics.com)

Next we see that Albertson's Inc. (ABS), the food store chain, has declined more than 11 percent on a day when the markets in general are very quiet. Although the New Home Sales report could potentially impact consumer buying at the company's stores, the stock story itself seems to be the main influence on its price. In late August or early September 2005, ABS announced it had hired Goldman Sachs to assist it with private offers for the firm. The stock moved higher on such a prospect and has had a variety of news stories on the subject since. Today's news indicates the company is no longer looking at a sale of the entire business, but will entertain sales of underperforming groups. It appears Wall Street did not like the prospect of the company remaining public, as the low-margin industry is facing more competition from Wal-Mart and other discount chains entering the business.

Given the minimal impact of economic reports on the markets as a whole, it seems reasonable to conclude that the decline in ABS shares is largely due to the company news released. Although the negative consumer report may have amplified the impact of the news, a look at the price of ABS competitor Safeway (SWY—down 0.16 percent) suggests it is all about the news story. The strong downward move in the stock may also indicate that news of this change in corporate planning did not leak out to other parties prior to hitting the news wires.

VOCABULARY DEFINITIONS

Buying pressure: In terms of the TICK, buying pressure is used to describe a bullish situation where increased demand (or decreased supply) is reflected in an increasing TICK level.

Contagion: A global sell-off in financial markets.

Discount rate: The rate at which the Federal Reserve lends money to member banks.

Downtick: When the most recent trade on a stock occurs at a lower price than the prior trade, the stock is on a downtick.

Efficient Market Theory: According to one school of thought, it isn't possible to successfully trade the market because the arrival of new information is very quickly incorporated into asset prices. Only new information can move stock prices; since the future is completely unpredictable, it follows that stock prices are erratic or random.

Federal Reserve: Created by Congress in 1913, the Federal Reserve consists of 12 district banks as well as a Board of Governors. The primary goals of the Federal Reserve are to stabilize prices, promote economic growth, and strive for full employment.

Fed funds rate: The rate that Federal Reserve member banks impose upon one another for overnight loans.

Index fund: A passively managed fund that seeks to match the performance of the index on which it is based. These types of funds often outperform active funds and are a low-cost investment option.

Institutional investors: Large investors who make investment decisions on behalf of clients or customers. They include mutual fund managers, pension fund managers, hedge fund managers, and financial advisers. The large-scale buying and selling from these investors will move stock prices.

Passive investing: Passive investing seeks only to match the performance of the market; it involves no decision making. This type of investing can be accomplished via index funds designed to track the performance of a specific index.

Portfolio insurance: Portfolio insurance programs allow large investors to sell off large portions of their stocks when certain parameters of an insurance model are met.

Program trading: The simultaneous purchase or sale of 15 or more stocks worth more than $1 million.

Random walker: A follower of the Efficient Market Theory.

Retail investor: An investor who makes investment decisions for his own accounts. Retail investors are not paid to make investment decisions and do so only for their own gain.

Selling pressure: In terms of the TICK, selling pressure is used to describe a bearish situation where decreased demand (or increased supply) is reflected in a decreasing TICK level.

Tick: A movement in the price or quote of a security or contract.

Uptick: When the most recent trade on a stock occurs at a higher price than the prior trade, the stock is on an uptick.

CHAPTER 9

System Trading

SUMMARY

System trading is one approach to the markets that removes an individual's biases and emotions. It is a form of trading that identifies strict rules for entry and exit; there is no decision making for the trader once the system's wheels are set in motion. Flexibility is added to the system by varying the indicator speeds or timing, or by incorporating additional criteria known as filters.

In its purest form, a trading system is completely automated. The system generates a buy signal that then generates a buy order in the trader's account. When a signal to close the position is generated by the system, the sell order to close is also generated. While we are not advocating that readers set up such a system and put their brokerage account on autopilot, we are suggesting traders seriously consider exploring trading systems so they can benefit from their greatest advantage: taking emotion out of the trade.

True system trading requires backtesting the signals over a sufficiently long period of time. It is important to monitor results over a variety of market conditions—bullish, bearish, and neutral. There are charting packages available (such as ProfitSource) that have built-in system scanning and testing features, making this step in the process much more efficient than ever. Once a trader has developed a logical system, tested it, and found the results satisfactory, he should be able to move forward with the system in confidence.

Not all traders will choose to use the same systems; like options, the variety in both is extensive. The first review of a system's results will measure such factors as maximum drawdown, average winning trade, average losing trade, and percent profitable. A system needs to prove itself to be effective first and foremost. The next step for the trader is to determine whether the system is suitable for his or her needs. One consideration is whether the equity requirements for the system are in line with the trader's assets. Like any trade approach, system trading has its strengths, but it does not represent the market's holy grail to profits. It is a tool for the individual that readily fits into an index approach to trading.

QUESTIONS AND EXERCISES

1. A trading system _____ use a specific set of trading rules for entry and exit.
   A. Does.
   B. Does not.

2. If a trader can discipline himself to follow a system, with rigor, _____ will not rule the decision-making process.
   A. Losses.
   B. Discipline.
   C. Emotions.
   D. Rationality.

3. The 10 stocks in the Dow Jones Industrial Average with the highest dividend yields are referred to as the _____.
   A. Dow Mutts.
   B. High 10 Yielders.
   C. Way to profits.
   D. Dogs of the Dow.

4. True or false: Due to the strictness required in system trading, the trader has no ability to introduce flexibility into this approach.

5. The _____ represents a range that is based on one of three calculated values.

   A. True range.
   B. Average true range.
   C. Absolute range.
   D. Complete range.

6. True or false: The Dogs of the Dow strategy is strictly a short-term trading strategy.

7. Match the system statistic term with its definition by placing the proper number in the space provided.

   A. Average winning trade (AWT)   _____   1. AWT / ALT
   B. Average losing trade (ALT)   _____   2. Reduction in equity due to a losing trade.
   C. Win-to-loss ratio   _____   3. Losing trades $ amount/ # of losing trades.
   D. Drawdown   _____   4. Winning trades $ amount / # of winning trades.
   E. Maximum drawdown   _____   5. Cumulative equity reduction from losing trades.

8. The Volex system uses _____ to create _____ the current day's high and low prices.

   A. An ATR multiple / the average of.
   B. An ATR multiple / bands around.
   C. Volatility / bands around.
   D. Bands / volatility around.

9. A price break to the upside, penetrating the _____, generates a long buy signal in the Volex system.

   A. Average true range.
   B. True range.
   C. Upper Volex band.
   D. Lower Volex band.

10. True or false: The revised Volex system uses a point and figure reversal exit.

11. The average win-to-loss ratio should be a minimum of _____.
    A. 2:1.
    B. 1:2.
    C. 3:1.
    D. 1:3.

12. The term used to describe an additional system parameter that seeks to improve trade entry and exit is a(n) _____.
    A. Efficiency indicator.
    B. Filter.
    C. Drawdown tool.
    D. Valuable thing.

13. True or false: Systems with initial poor results should be discarded.

14. A robust system is _____ and _____.
    A. Consistent / useful across multiple markets.
    B. Profitable / optimized.
    C. Trade intensive / optimized.
    D. Low-cost / profitable.

15. True or false: It is useful to establish stop-loss levels based on initial system tests.

MEDIA ASSIGNMENT

The media assignment for Chapter 9 requires the reader to develop a *very simple* system using market data for one week. The data can be accessed via the Internet or a daily business journal. Your local newspaper may also provide sufficient information. The focus for this assignment is more process than the end result.

It is highly unlikely that the system created by observing one week's data will be one that you actually put into use as a trader. Don't discount the effort, though. Developing a trading system and testing it can be a pretty sizable new challenge; this will help you create smaller steps to get you going once you are ready to move forward in earnest.

Review market data for one week, including broad market averages, sector indexes, and ETFs. Note any trends observed by using both index level data and volume data, along with any other indicator you can access each day. Such an observation can include consecutive day type observations (i.e., what happens when the market is up x consecutive days) or day of the week type observations. Develop a simple trading system that will be profitable based on the observed trend. You can use any appropriate ETF or option strategy, but you must identify specific entry and exit rules. Keep in mind that system exits can be time specific, based on specific moves for the underlying (including stop-losses), or based on other indicators.

Again, the focus for this exercise is on process. All of the work can be completed in a trading notebook—no programming or computer access is required.

VOCABULARY LIST

Alert	Maximum drawdown
Average losing trade	Maximum favorable excursion
Average true range (ATR)	Parameter
Average winning trade	Percent profitable
Average win-to-loss ratio	Roundtrip
Backtesting	System
Discretionary trader	System trader
Drawdown	True range (TR)
Filter	Volatility
Gap	Volex system
Maximum adverse excursion	Volex trading bands

SOLUTIONS

1. A trading system _____ use a specific set of trading rules for entry and exit.

   Answer: A—Does.

   Discussion: A trading system is defined for our purposes as a trade approach that does have specific rules for trade entry and exit. This can include an automated system or a system that is executed manually by the trader. Discretionary trading, while less specific for entry and exit, still requires a plan to manage risk.

2. If a trader can discipline himself to follow a system, with rigor, _____ will not rule the decision-making process.

   Answer: C—Emotions.

   Discussion: Although more experienced traders may be able to better control the impact their emotions have on trading, all traders are subject to feelings of greed and fear when involved in a trade. The best way to manage such emotions is to execute a system with discipline.

3. The 10 stocks in the Dow Jones Industrial Average with the highest dividend yields are referred to as the _____.

   Answer: D—Dogs of the Dow.

   Discussion: The Dogs of the Dow strategy, described by Michael O'Higgins in his book *Beating the Dow*, is an annually rebalanced trade approach. It categorizes the year's 10 top-yielding Dow stocks as the Dogs of the Dow. These stocks are kept in a portfolio until the next year's rebalancing. The $MUT Index is a CBOE product that tracks these top 10 Dow components.

4. True or false: Due to the strictness required in system trading, the trader has no ability to introduce flexibility into this approach.

   Answer: False.

   Discussion: Flexibility is introduced to a trading system by varying indicator speeds and adding filters. Since the number of such variations is limitless, a great deal of flexibility can be built into a system.

5. The _____ represents a range that is based on one of three calculated values.

   Answer: A—True range.

   Discussion: The true range, developed by Welles Wilder, is a measure of volatility that incorporates price gaps into a moving average calculation. The indicator defines the range by using the greatest of three calculated values: (1) the current high minus the current low, (2) the current high minus the previous close, or (3) the current low minus the previous close. In general, if the difference between the high and low of the day is large, that value will be used to compute the day's true range. When the difference between the high and low is small, one of the other two methods might define the true range.

6. True or false: The Dogs of the Dow strategy is strictly a short-term trading strategy.

   Answer: False.

   Discussion: As discussed in question 4, the Dogs of the Dow is a trade approach that creates a portfolio that is intact for one year. As a result, this system is well suited for traders seeking a long-term strategy.

7. Match the term with its definition by placing the proper number in the space provided.

   Answer:

   A. Average winning trade (AWT)—4. Winning trades $ amount / # of winning trades.

   B. Average losing trades (ALT)—3. Losing trades $ amount / # of losing trades.

   C. Win-to-loss ratio—1. AWT / ALT.

   D. Drawdown—2. Reduction in equity due to a losing trade.

   E. Maximum drawdown—5. Cumulative equity reduction from losing trades.

8. The Volex system uses _____ to create _____ the current day's high and low prices.

   Answer: B—An ATR multiple / bands around.

   Discussion: The Volex system has a slightly more complex indicator construction, but one that is still manageable. Rather than creating bands around one set value, Volex uses the upper end of the period's price range to serve as a base for the upper Volex band and the lower end of the period's price range to serve as a base for the lower Volex band. The value that is added and subtracted, respectively, to construct the bands is based on the ATR, specifically (ATR × cATR), where c is some user-defined constant value.

9. A price break to the upside, penetrating the _____, generates a long buy signal in the Volex system.

   Answer: C—Upper Volex band.

   Discussion: The Volex system seeks to enter a long position when price moves upward past a standard level of volatility that is constructed by using the product of the ATR and a user-defined constant multiplied by the ATR. This volatility level is represented by a band that is constructed by adding (ATR × cATR) to the current high for the security. When price penetrates the upper band, further upward price action is expected and the trader should enter a long position.

10. True or false: The revised Volex system uses a point and figure reversal exit.

    Answer: True.

    Discussion: The original Volex system, developed by Bill Cruz and Charlie Wright, uses the band opposite the entry band (upper band for long positions) to exit a trade. When a trader is long the market, penetration of the lower Volex band signals trade exit and a closing of the long position. The revised system used by Tom Gentile incorporates a three-box point and figure reversal to trade exit.

11. The average win-to-loss ratio should be a minimum of _____.

    Answer: A—2:1.

    Discussion: The average win-to-loss ratio, which is calculated by dividing the average wins by the average losses, should be a minimum of 2:1. When profits outpace losses by a factor of two, systems do not need to be right more than 50 percent of the time. The key is to create a system that allows profits to run while cutting losses. Incorporating reasonable system-dictated stop-losses is one method that can be used to help achieve this goal.

12. The term used to describe an additional system parameter that seeks to improve trade entry and exit is a(n) _____.

Answer: B—Filter.

Discussion: The question defines a system filter. An example of such a system parameter is a rising ADX line that is above 20, which signals a trending period. The goal of adding this filter is to minimize false signals for a trend-following system.

13. True or false: Systems with initial poor results should be discarded.

Answer: False.

Discussion: If the basis for the system is valid, there are steps that can be taken to improve the performance of initial results. An important criterion for proceeding in such a manner is consistent results that can be measured by the standard deviation of trade returns. In the event a particularly poor performer is encountered, the trader may want to reverse the buy and sell signals generated, providing such a step is logical. It is rare for a trader to establish certain parameters and indicator speeds as a first cut and have this system immediately be usable. It takes time to develop a usable system, from both the system perspective and the developer experience perspective.

14. A robust system is _____ and _____.

Answer: A—Consistent / useful across multiple markets.

Discussion: Although we seek to develop profitable systems, one that is robust also provides consistent results and is valid across multiple securities and markets. Consistency can be measured by evaluating the standard deviation (SD) of returns. A lower SD value translates to more stable returns and a more stable system.

15. True or false: It is useful to establish stop-loss levels based on initial system tests.

Answer: True.

Discussion: Although all traders need to identify maximum loss levels for their trading, a system should be able to generate its own logical stop area. A stop we develop for risk management is arbitrary when put in the context of a trading system. Once a system-dictated stop is generated, the newly revised system should be tested with this stop in place. The trader should then review the results to determine whether the risk inherent in the system falls within the trader's risk parameters.

MEDIA ASSIGNMENT

The system trading media assignment is relatively light in terms of accessing new information through media, but it requires the reader to analyze the regularly available information differently. The reader is to review market data for a one-week period and develop a simple trading system based on this very small period of time. (*Note:* Before attempting to use a system created with such limited data, it would need to be significantly backtested first.)

Using the market week beginning Monday, December 12, the information in Figure 9.1 includes the closing data noted during the review. This kind of information is readily available from web sites or newspapers, including many local papers.

	Mo12			Tu13			We14			Th15			Fr16 (option expiration)		
	Price	Ch%	Vol	Price	Ch%	Vol	Price	Ch%	Vol	Price	Ch%	Vol	Price	Ch%	Vol
$INDU	10767.8	-0.10%	2541297	10823.7	0.52%	3290454	10883.5	0.55%	3364427	10881.7	-0.02%	2975573	10875.6	-0.06%	4190366
DIA	107.72	-0.02%	50962	108.39	0.62%	77312	109.00	0.56%	70454	108.77	-0.21%	84615	108.51	-0.24%	45731
$SPX	1260.43	0.08%	14063	1267.43	0.56%	17754	1272.74	0.42%	16361	1270.94	-0.14%	16090	1267.32	-0.28%	20842
SPY	126.45	0.09%	483938	127.31	0.68%	886472	127.81	0.39%	643744	127.44	-0.29%	559027	126.36	-0.85%	462390
$NDX	1638.35	0.34%	170541	1706.77	0.44%	19341	1698.98	-0.40%	17658	1701.70	0.16%	18236	1688.68	-0.77%	25548
QQQQ	41.87	0.36%	448700	42.05	0.43%	766116	41.90	-0.36%	750865	41.97	0.17%	726782	41.58	-0.93%	637413

FIGURE 9.1 Weekly Market Results, December 12–16, 2005 (*Source:* www .Optionetics.com)

Assuming that this week is representative of typical option expiration weeks, we note that a marginally lower close in the Dow Jones Industrials ($INDU) the day before expiration for equity options precedes a marginally lower close in the index the next day (option expiration). Further, the impact is amplified in the diamonds (DIA), which is the ETF that tracks the Dow 30.

Based on this observation, it is *assumed* (big assumption here) that when the $INDU closes down marginally the Thursday before expiration, it will continue down the next day. This same trend occurs in DIA. A trading system aimed at capturing the one-day decline in DIA is developed. Since the actual movement in the ETF is relatively small, the system will make use of the ETF itself rather than options on the ETF, which may not realize a significant movement in the limited period of time.

The following system was created for this exercise (but not implemented):

Strategy: DIA Monthly Expiration System, capture continued downward movement in DIA on expiration Friday when the INDU Index and DIA ETF close lower the day prior to expiration.

- **Entry Rule:** Enter a $2,000 short position in DIA at the close of trading the day before (usually Thursday) DIA options' last trading day prior to expiration (usually Friday).
- **Exit Rule:** Close the DIA position by buying back the DIA shares at the close the next day or if the shares climb more than 1 percent during the day.

The second part of the exit provides additional protection in the event the market rallies the next day, but it will not protect against a large gap open since a position is held overnight. The best way to establish the stop-loss percentage is to review past data and note the intraday DIA percentage gains on months the entry signal would have triggered, while still resulting in a decline on the day. Needless to say, quite a bit of other testing would need to be completed, but the basic system is consistent with the observed trend and the strategy employed to take advantage of it is valid.

VOCABULARY DEFINITIONS

Alert: A technical condition that provides a trader with a warning about a pending signal or change in conditions.

Average losing trade: A trading system statistic that represents the average loser of all the losing trades generated by the system. It is the total number of dollars divided by the number of losing trades.

Average true range (ATR): The moving average of the true range (TR).

Average winning trade: A trading system statistic that represents the average winner of all the winning trades generated by the system. It is computed as the dollar amount of all winning trades divided by the number of winning trades.

Average win-to-loss ratio: A trading system statistic that is calculated by dividing the average dollar amount of winners by the average dollar amount of losers.

Backtesting: The process used by system traders to apply a system to historic prices.

Discretionary trader: A trader who makes decisions as events unfold and based on new information. The discretionary trader is more likely to make decisions based on hunches, guesswork, and emotion.

Drawdown: The value of the reduction in equity for an account due to a losing trade.

Filter: A trading rule or system parameter. This additional trade requirement seeks to minimize entry and exit from false signals to improve profitability.

Gap: A void at certain price levels on a technical chart, caused by a move up (or down) in price that exceeds the previous period's high (or low).

Maximum adverse excursion: The largest loss per position based on a percentage of the initial trade size. This value is an unrealized value—it does not reflect the actual trade exit.

Maximum drawdown: A trading system statistic that represents the sum of the most consecutive losers generated. It is the largest drawdown for the account when the system is tested (or put into use).

Maximum favorable excursion: The largest gain per position based on a percentage of the initial trade size. This value is an unrealized value—it does not reflect the actual trade exit.

Parameter: A rule for a trading system. An example of a parameter includes an ADX value that is above 20 and rising.

Percent profitable: A trading system statistic that measures the probability of the system generating profitable trades.

Roundtrip: When evaluating the costs for a system, trades can be described as one-way (entry only) or roundtrip (entry and exit).

System: In trading, a set of strictly followed rules for trade entry and exit.

System trader: A trader who uses specific rules for getting in and out of the market with a systems approach that he is comfortable with and therefore is able to execute without emotion getting in the way.

True range (TR): The greatest of the following:
- Current high less the current low.
- The absolute value of the current high less the previous close.
- The absolute value of the current low less the previous close.

Volatility: A statistical measure of the tendency of a market or security to rise or fall sharply within a period of time.

Volex system: A trading system that uses volatility to forecast change in price.

Volex trading bands: Bands created by the Volex system around the average true range, a specified distance apart.

Getting an Edge with Indicators

SUMMARY

Looking for bullish or bearish trends is only one step toward creating profitable strategies—the trader needs to gain a sense of the sustainability of the trend as well. The market indicators covered in Chapter 10 are designed to help the trader with such an assessment. Included in this chapter is a discussion of market internals and sentiment indicators, along with other tools to assist the reader in gaining a trading edge.

Although not always considered the most glamorous of indicators, volume cannot be overlooked. Traders should recognize the source of data for volume readings (by security or by exchange) and use exchange and index-based readings to their fullest advantage. Separating volume into up volume and down volume and examining volume associated with advancers and decliners helps make the health of a move more apparent. Important market internals to assist with this effort are market breadth readings and the Arms Index for various exchanges (i.e., TRIN for the NYSE).

In addition to weakening market internals, a move will become suspect when certain sentiment indicators reach extreme readings. Put-to-call (P/C) ratios are important tools in this area of analysis; keep in mind, however, that not all P/C ratios are the same. Understanding the data underlying this statistic is necessary in order to use the tools correctly. Consider adding newer readings such as the International Security Exchange's (ISE) sentiment measurement and Bollinger's Put Volume Indicator to augment your analysis with traditional, long-standing ratios.

Sentiment analysts also make use of sentiment surveys, equity mutual fund data, and short interest data to better understand whether a market has become overextended. The strategist can evaluate crowd psychology moving the market upward or downward by considering the relative measure of these different tools—it is atypical for a specific indicator value to sound an alarm across trading floors. Experience will help the trader with such a nuance.

Other market dynamics traders should understand to gain an edge include seasonal factors and market anomalies. Reversals that appear to be materializing in late October may be given more merit by the strategist who knows that the November through May period is generally bullish. An experienced strategist further recognizes that such a seasonal tendency is not a rule; the market can move any way it chooses. When a market participant becomes receptive to the myriad tools available, and puts a plan in place to use these tools in a manner consistent with his or her own style, he or she is on the way to gaining that market edge we all seek.

QUESTIONS AND EXERCISES

1. Strong volume on a decline _____ confirm the bearish trend.

   A. Does.

   B. Does not.

2. Subsequent rallies during a trend that is predominantly downward should occur on _____ volume.

   A. Heavier.

   B. Lighter.

   C. Similar.

   D. Rational.

3. Surges in volume that occur at important turning points are known as blow-off _____ and _____.
   A. Reversals / tops.
   B. Tops / bottoms.
   C. Reversals / spikes.
   D. Reversals / profit points.

4. True or false: A trader may seek to improve system results by using stop-losses or identifying a specific number of days to exit the trade when losses are not otherwise limited.

5. The _____ is an important market breadth tool that provides insight to market internals.
   A. True market range.
   B. Dow weekly closing value.
   C. Weekly closing value for the Dow Industrials, NASDAQ, and S&P 500.
   D. Advance / decline line.

6. The numerator for the TRIN (a.k.a. Arms Index) incorporates the volume of declining securities divided by the number of _____ securities.
   A. Declining.
   B. Advancing.
   C. Flat.
   D. Total.

7. Match the market anomaly or sentiment indicator with its definition by placing the proper number in the space provided.

   A. Value Line enigma _____
   B. Size effect
   C. Low P/E effect _____
   D. ISEE
   E. CBOE put-to-call ratio

   1. A put-to-call ratio with new purchases only.
   2. A put-to-call ratio skewed by selling transactions.
   3. An anomaly that counters EMT.
   4. A market capitalization anomaly.
   5. A company fundamental anomaly.

8. True or false: The new high–new low (NHNL) index is a tool to gauge internal market strength, with a declining NHNL index signaling weakness.

9. True or false: Neither the Titanic Syndrome nor the Hindenburg Omen has yielded a false signal in the 40 years that they have been tracked.

10. Which types of tools focus on fundamental factors relating to different categories of companies?
    A. Breadth readings.
    B. Market anomalies.
    C. Market enigmas.
    D. Analyst sentiment.

11. The Value Line stock ranking system incorporates all but the following into its analysis:
    A. Technical indicators.
    B. Earnings momentum.
    C. Analyst sentiment.
    D. Risk.

12. The traditional use of the CBOE put-to-call (P/C) ratio incorporates the monitoring of readings that are _____.
    A. Extreme.
    B. Greater than 1.0.
    C. Less than 1.0.
    D. Below a zero line.

13. True or false: The CBOE P/C ratio calculates the number of equity-only puts relative to equity-only calls on all six exchanges.

14. The _____ put-to-call ratio generally reflects what smart money is doing and as a result is a confirming rather than contrarian tool.
    A. CBOE Equity.
    B. CBOE VIX.
    C. INDU.
    D. OEX.

15. The _____ was constructed by one of the newer options exchanges and reflects purchases rather than total option volumes.

    A. Boston Option Exchange's Sentiment (BOXs).

    B. International Securities Sentiment Index (ISEE).

    C. Philadelphia Stock Exchange's P/C Ratio (PHLX).

    D. Maher's Politically Correct Sentiment (M-PCS).

16. True or false: The Bollinger PVI measures the relative level of put activity and is calculated by using current-day put volume divided by the 10-day moving average of put volume.

17. According to Alexander Elder in his book *Trading for a Living*, the _____ class of futures traders tends to be the most reliable when following the Commitments of Traders report.

    A. Small speculator.

    B. Large speculator.

    C. Commercial hedger.

    D. Smart money.

18. True or false: According to the Maximum Pain Theory (MPT), the price of an underlying asset will gravitate toward the point where the greatest number of options expire worthless at expiration.

MEDIA ASSIGNMENT

The media assignment for this chapter requires the reader to access a television or radio program that focuses on the markets. The goal is to listen to the types of analysis being provided and distinguish each as fundamental, technical, or sentiment analysis. Some programming is more focused than others, but ideally you'll be able to capture glimpses of a variety of analytical forms. Many brokerage offices provide cable business programming during business hours and it is not uncommon to find market-oriented radio programming near the open and close of the market.

In addition to identifying the type of analysis being completed, decide for yourself the bearing the information has on your type of trading and to what extent you believe the topic strongly supports its point. As an example, a commentator may mention that the stock market is down because the price of oil is up. While the price of oil may certainly impact the stock market, is this a sufficient explanation of what is driving prices? There is an inflationary aspect (fundamental) but also a crowd psychology aspect (sentiment) to this one-line explanation of the market day.

A very important word of caution: Keep in mind that some shows have very extended hours and need to create programming content. This is not to say that the news is being fabricated, but it can be difficult to separate what is important from what is not important if you don't listen with a discerning ear. Remember that like any other news piece, there is a certain element of tugging at human emotions. This is something traders seek to minimize. So again, be wary of the impact this exercise has on your plan.

VOCABULARY LIST

Advance/decline line

Advance/decline ratio

Advancing issues

Arms Index (also TRIN)

Blow-off top

Bollinger Put Volume Indicator (PVI)

Commitments of Traders report (COT)

Contrarian

Declining issues

Down volume

Hindenburg Omen

International Securities Sentiment Index (ISEE)

Investment Company Institute (ICI)

Investment survey

January barometer

January effect

Low P/E effect

Market anomaly

Market breadth

Market internals

Maximum Pain Theory (MPT)

Mutual fund cash assets percentage

Mutual funds flows

New high–new low (NHNL) index

OEX put-to-call ratio

Presidential election cycle

Price-to-dividend

Put-to-call ratio

Seasonal pattern

Selling climax

Sentiment analysis

Sentiment indicator

Short interest

Size effect

Smart money

Titanic Syndrome

TRIN (also Arms Index)

Up volume

Value Line enigma

Volume

SOLUTIONS

1. Strong volume on a decline _____ confirm the bearish trend.

   Answer: A—Does.

   Discussion: Rising volume confirms the existing trend, whether it is upward or downward. Anytime a bearish market phase is in place, look to volume divergences as an early alert to potential changes in the trend.

2. Subsequent rallies during a trend that is predominantly downward should occur on _____ volume.

   Answer: B—Lighter.

   Discussion: When a downward trend remains intact, attempts for the market to move higher are often accompanied by light volume. New buyers remain skeptical that the upward price action is sustainable—they have not yet reached a point where they fear missing a rally. Sellers are easily able to meet the limited demand of buyers, fearful that declines will return while they remain long.

3. Surges in volume that occur at important turning points are known as blow-off _____ and _____.

   Answer: B—Tops / bottoms.

   Discussion: Although volume is expected to increase in the direction of the trend, increasingly strong rising volume suggests that fear and greed are significant drivers in the move. When volume surges in a blow-off bottom, investors who are willing to supply shares at low prices run dry sooner rather than later. The same is true when price runs up quickly—the demand peak happens quickly, signaling a potential end to the trend.

4. True or false: A trader may seek to improve system results by using stop-losses or identifying a specific number of days to exit the trade when losses are not otherwise limited.

    Answer: True.

    Discussion: Trading systems are very flexible given the large variety of entry and exit parameters available. When a particular approach caps profits, the trader will need to also cap losses through a percentage move signal or time-in-trade signal. Without such a filter, profits will be limited while losses are permitted to run—the exact opposite of how we seek to benefit from a system.

5. The _____ is an important market breadth tool that provides insight to market internals.

    Answer: D—Advance/decline line.

    Discussion: One of the most widely used breadth tools is the advance/decline line, which subtracts the number of decliners from advancers for a particular exchange. The trend of this line is evaluated to determine if it supports (confirms) existing market action or serves as a warning about its strength. Another popular breadth tool is the advance/decline ratio.

6. The numerator for the TRIN (a.k.a. Arms Index) incorporates the volume of declining securities divided by the number of _____ securities.

    Answer: A—Declining.

    Discussion: By definition, the TRIN is calculated as follows:

$$\text{TRIN} = \frac{(\text{Volume for decliners/\# Decliners})}{(\text{Volume for advancers/\# Advancers})}$$

7. Match the market anomaly or sentiment indicator with its definition by placing the proper number in the space provided.

    Answer:

    A. Value Line enigma—3. An anomaly that counters EMT.

    B. Size effect—4. A market capitalization anomaly.

    C. Low P/E effect—5. A company fundamental anomaly.

    D. ISEE—1. A put-to-call ratio with new purchases only.

    E. CBOE put-to-call ratio—2. A put-to-call ratio skewed by selling transactions.

8. True or false: The new high–new low (NHNL) index is a tool to gauge internal market strength, with a declining NHNL Index signaling weakness.

   Answer: True.

   Discussion: The NHNL Index is constructed by subtracting the number of new 52-week highs from the number of new 52-week lows. When there are more new highs, the number is positive. A string of positive readings, or rising index line, is bullish. Conversely, when new lows are steadily increasing, the line is declining and the market is weakening.

9. True or false: Neither the Titanic Syndrome nor the Hindenburg Omen has yielded a false signal in the 40 years that they have been tracked.

   Answer: False.

   Discussion: Traders can never assume that an indicator signal is always right and will continue to be right in the future. The only thing that is ever right is the market itself. As certain well-performing tools gain popularity, their effectiveness may diminish. This is not to say that they will completely lose their functionality, but the readings needed to generate a signal may become skewed or they may fall in and out of favor with the masses. The best way to combat such an effect on tools you find useful is to have a variety of them at your disposal. When a few of these are favoring a certain assessment, you are increasing your probability of reading the market correctly.

10. Which types of tools focus on fundamental factors relating to different categories of companies?

    Answer: B—Market anomalies.

    Discussion: A market anomaly is defined as a fundamental factor that affects the markets and offers sector opportunities in a group of securities for improved performance. Market anomalies include such factors as the capitalization size effect, the low P/E effect, and the Value Line enigma, among others.

11. The Value Line stock ranking system incorporates all but the following into its analysis:

    Answer: C—Analyst sentiment.

    Discussion: Value Line ranking is said to include earnings momentum, technical indicators, and certain company risk factors in its analysis of securities. The consistent outperformance of this ranking system is counter to efficient market theory, which postulates that such a performance is not possible. Although security analysts who provide buy, hold, and sell recommendations may use criteria similar to Value Line's, their analysis is not part of the Value Line ranking.

12. The traditional use of the CBOE put-to-call (P/C) ratio incorporates the monitoring of readings that are: _____.

    Answer: A—Extreme.

    Discussion: Sentiment analysis generally requires users to monitor relative movements in their tools rather than exact readings. *Extreme readings* itself is a relative term—what can be extreme for one index (i.e., OEX) may be more calm for another group of securities (i.e., CBOE equity-only P/C ratio). Through study and experience the analyst will gain a greater understanding of how to gauge these readings.

13. True or false: The CBOE P/C ratio calculates the number of equity-only puts relative to equity-only calls on all six exchanges.

    Answer: False.

    Discussion: The CBOE P/C ratio calculates the number of equity and index puts relative to equity and index calls on the CBOE only. Although quite a bit of information is provided in this chapter, hopefully the reader will recognize that there is a ton of data to evaluate in a number of different ways. In some cases a trader may need to seek it out and work the numbers a bit, and in other instances it is readily available. By accessing the Options Clearing Corporation data (www.optionsclearing.com), strategists can create P/C ratios for all options exchanges.

14. The _____ put-to-call ratio generally reflects what smart money is doing and as a result is a confirming rather than contrarian tool.

    Answer: D—OEX.

    Discussion: The OEX P/C ratio is a tool for quantifying relative levels of bullish or bearish sentiment using OEX options trading information. Unlike the total and equity P/C ratios, the OEX P/C ratio should not be used as a contrarian tool since the traders involved in this market are considered more sophisticated and a bit more adept at timing the market. This may be due to the generally higher premium (cost) of index options as opposed to equity options.

15. The _____ was constructed by one of the newer options exchanges and reflects purchases rather than total option volumes.

    Answer: B—International Securities Sentiment Index (ISEE).

    Discussion: The International Securities Exchange's ISEE indicator improves the put-to-call ratio by limiting the analysis to puts and calls that have been bought throughout the trading day. Options that have been sold are not included in the equation. Despite a relatively short track record, the sentiment index does a pretty good job of highlighting extreme levels of bullish or bearish sentiment.

16. True or false: The Bollinger PVI measures the relative level of put activity and is calculated by using current-day put volume divided by the 10-day moving average of put volume.

    Answer: True.

    Discussion: As defined in Chapter 10, the Bollinger Put Volume Indicator measures relative levels of put activity and can be applied to an individual stock, a specific index like the S&P 100 ($OEX), or an entire exchange. It is a contrarian indicator that is computed by accessing put option volume history. It divides the current period's put volume by the 10-period moving average of that put volume. A reading of 2.00 tells us that the period's put volume—and bearish sentiment—is two times greater than average. Low readings, on the other hand, indicate relatively high levels of bullishness or complacency among investors.

17. According to Alexander Elder in his book *Trading for a Living*, the _____ class of futures traders tends to be the most reliable when following the Commitments of Traders Report.

    Answer: C—Commercial hedgers.

    Discussion: In looking for signs of shifting sentiment, Alexander Elder suggests following the commercial traders because their decisions are well-informed since they have significant risk at stake. In his book *Trading for a Living*, he says that big speculators today are "trend following behemoths" and "do poorly as a group." Furthermore, "The masses of small traders are proverbial 'wrong-way Corrigans' of the markets."

18. True or false: According to the Maximum Pain Theory (MPT), the price of an underlying asset will gravitate toward the point where the greatest number of options expire worthless at expiration.

    Answer: True.

    Discussion: Maximum Pain is an observed phenomenon that an underlying asset will gravitate toward the point where the greatest number of options will be worthless at expiration whether due to market manipulation or mere chance. In order to compute the maximum pain price, or the price level that will see the greatest number of options expire worthless, the first step is to compute the dollar value of all open contracts. This process is described in detail toward the end of the chapter.

MEDIA ASSIGNMENT

This media assignment makes use of a different but accessible tool, business news programming. As luck would have it, portions of this book are being written near the end of 2005, bringing some seasonal factors to the forefront of the news. CNBC was easily accessible and left on for a few hours before the market close. There was quite a bit of analysis discussed—something for everyone, as it were. While we are wary of the impact such programming has on the emotions, we noted that the coverage from this focused cable program provided a nice variety of approaches to the markets—there were traders on the floor, sector and security fundamental analysts, economists, and other market participants.

Rather than getting into every topic viewed, we cover a couple of items here as they relate to this chapter. The amount of content provided in a relatively short period of time reminds us of an important adage: Beware of analysis paralysis. That said, let's continue to the exercise at hand.

A big topic in year-end programming is forecasts for the coming year, along with reviewing the previous year. Like in a baseball game, there are lots of statistics that can be accessed along the way. In terms of forecasts, the missing Santa Claus rally and what it means for the January barometer was mentioned. These seasonal tendencies are easily categorized as market anomalies, and we note that while Santa Claus rallies often occur, an absence of one is definitely not cause to load up on index puts in a bearish overreaction. Recall that although the last week of 2004 closed moderately up, it was followed by a rough January.

In addition to this mention of some seasonal patterns in the broadcast, two big fundamental topics were part of the forecast: the price of two key commodities (oil and gold) for 2006 and market capitalization forecasts. As mentioned earlier, rising oil prices drive inflationary fears, which often decreases market prices as the crowd reacts to the news. The longer-term fundamental impact takes on a shorter-term valuation view that is driven by sentiment. Other discussions included the argument for big caps over small caps in one story and the argument for small caps over big caps in another. The reasoning behind each seemed compelling, leading us to lean toward a review of 2004 to see where momentum seemed best for the earlier part of the year. In this instance, sound fundamental logic brings us to a technical review for further insight. It seems safe to say there will likely be winners and losers in both types of securities.

Finally, throughout the day, charts of individual securities, ETFs, sectors, and broad averages were displayed from a short-term basis through longer-term ones. A variety of basic indicators were used (technical analysis). Along with this commentary, traders and floor reporters commented on market breadth and sentiment. As stated earlier, there really was something for everyone.

Hopefully one of the conclusions you draw from this assignment is that many factors impact stock market prices. While we do not need to have an explanation for every twist and turn the market takes, we do need to have a sense of the prevailing trends, the strength of those trends, and how to construct a strategy that will take advantage of that outlook. Further, since the market alone will dictate what is next, we need to be prepared to manage our risk no matter how good a market assessment we complete.

VOCABULARY DEFINITIONS

Advance/decline line: Usually in reference to the New York Stock Exchange (NYSE), the advance/decline (A/D) line is calculated by subtracting the number of declining stocks from the number of advancing stocks on the NYSE each trading day. This measurement is a widely used gauge of market breadth and can also be calculated for other exchange breadth measurements.

Advance/decline ratio: Usually in reference to the NYSE, the advance/decline ratio is calculated by dividing the number of declining stocks from advancing stocks on the NYSE each trading day. Ratios of 2.5 or more indicate extremely positive market breadth and a bullish environment. This indicator can also be used for other exchange breadth measurements. Bullish traders should focus on the exchange where market breadth is showing the most strength or improvement.

Advancing issues: Stocks that have moved higher in price during a trading session. This value is generally reported by each exchange.

Arms Index (also TRIN): The Arms Index, named for its developer, Dick Arms, measures buying and selling pressure through the use of both advancing and declining statistics, along with volume statistics. See TRIN for the equation to calculate this ratio.

Blow-off top: A volume surge at top reversal—this is a bearish signal.

Bollinger Put Volume Indicator (PVI): The Bollinger PVI measures relative levels of put activity and is equal to the current day's put volume divided by the 10-day moving average (MA) of put volume. If the ratio rises, it indicates that put volume and bearish sentiment is on the rise. Similar to the put-to-call ratios, the indicator can be applied to an individual stock, a specific index, or to an entire exchange. It is another contrarian indicator.

Commitments of Traders report (COT): The Commodity Futures Trading Commission (CFTC) issues a report that breaks traders down for various contracts into three groups: small speculators, large speculators, and commercial hedgers. Large speculators are the ones that are holding certain position levels; commercials are firms or businesses that deal with commodities as part of their normal course of business activity; and small traders account for the remaining open interest.

Contrarian: An individual who uses sentiment indicators to take a view and position that is opposite to the crowd.

Declining issues: Stocks that have moved lower in price during a trading session. This value is generally reported by each exchange.

Down volume: The volume of stocks that are declining in price.

Hindenburg Omen: Created by Jim Miekka and popularized by Kennedy Gammage, the Hindenburg Omen is a somewhat complex indicator that forewarns of market crashes. It requires the following events to trigger a signal: (1) Both 52-week highs and 52-week lows are greater than 2.2 percent of all issues on the New York Stock Exchange; (2) the 10-week moving average of the NYSE Composite Index is trending higher; and (3) the McClellan Oscillator (a technical trading indicator) is in oversold territory. All of these factors suggest that although the market is trending higher, there is a significant amount of uncertainty and confusion—a situation that is ripe for a market crash.

International Securities Sentiment Index (ISEE): The ISEE is one of the newest sentiment tools used to track daily call and put activity on the International Securities Exchange (ISE), today's largest stock options exchange. It is similar in some ways to other exchange-specific put-to-call ratios, but is computed as the day's call activity divided by put activity, multiplied by 100. Therefore, the ISEE will fall when bearish sentiment increases and rise when bullishness is high. This index typically stays between 125 and 225. Another important difference between ISEE and the more widely used put-to-call ratio is that the ISEE measures only call and put purchases, rather than total volume.

Investment Company Institute (ICI): ICI is a company that provides data for the mutual fund industry. This information can also be used by sentiment analysts and includes mutual fund flow and percentage cash data.

Investment survey: Several services provide updates regarding investor sentiment from polls or surveys.

January barometer: A seasonal market theory that the stock market's performance during the month of January will determine its performance throughout the remainder of the year.

January effect: The seasonal tendency of small-cap stocks to outperform the larger-cap stocks from the end of December through January. The popularity of this seasonal effect has diminished its impact as traders seek to get ahead of the crowd earlier and earlier.

Low P/E effect: One of the oldest and best-documented anomalies, the low P/E effect indicates that stocks with low price-to-earnings (P/E) ratios tend to outperform the market over the long haul. Stocks with low price-to-book and price-to–cash flow ratios also outperform the market over the long term.

Market anomaly: A fundamental factor that affects the markets and offers opportunities in a group of securities for improved performance.

Market breadth: The term used to describe the general health of a market or exchange by evaluating the statistics for advancing issues versus statistics for declining issues on a particular exchange.

Market internals: The technical action of the market beyond the movement of the major averages. It includes such items as up and down volume, advancing and declining issues, and new highs and new lows.

Maximum Pain Theory (MPT): The tendency for the price of an underlying asset to gravitate toward the point where the greatest number of options expire worthless at expiration. According to Frederic Ruffy, determining the MPT point requires an analysis of the open interest for all options (puts and calls) associated with a specific underlying security.

Mutual fund cash assets percentage: Cash allocations in actively and passively managed mutual funds are reported as the mutual fund cash assets percentage. Severe market declines may lead to further decreases in prices when mutual fund investors remove shares from these investments, causing portfolio managers to sell additional stock due to minimal cash available in the fund.

Mutual fund flows: While mutual fund flows alone are not enough to push the stock market higher or lower, the flows do serve as an important source of liquidity. Robust inflows into stock funds serve as an important source of buying demand for the market. When the inflows slow or even turn into outflows, market volatility invariably increases.

New high–new low (NHNL) index: The NHNL Index compares the number of stocks setting new 52-week highs to the number of stocks setting new 52-week lows on a daily basis. It is calculated by subtracting the number of new lows from the number of new highs, by exchange. The index is used as a confirming tool, with a rising index confirming a rising market and a declining index confirming a declining market.

OEX put-to-call ratio: An index-specific put-to-call ratio used for sentiment analysis. When a large number of OEX puts are trading, it serves as an indication that the OEX traders are getting bearish, or hedging their bets. When OEX calls are more active than puts, OEX traders are predominantly bullish. The OEX P/C ratio is a tool for quantifying relative levels of bullish or bearish sentiment using OEX options trading information. This particular ratio is different from others in that OEX index traders as a whole are generally correct in predicting turning points. The OEX P/C ratio can be used to get clues regarding what the smart money is doing.

Presidential election cycle: A four-year seasonal cycle with bullish years occurring the year before and the year of the presidential election, likely due to the economic policy associated with the length of time an existing administration has been in place and the uncertainty around changes imposed by a new administration.

Price-to-dividend: A fundamental measurement that uses the dividend yield (annual dividends divided by price) to rank stocks. Those stocks that pay higher dividends tend to outperform the market over the longer term. According to David Dreman, a study including more than 25 years of data showed that stocks with the highest dividend yields outperformed the market by an average annual return of 1.2 percent. The superior gain was due in large part to the dividends themselves.

Put-to-call ratio: Generally referring to the Chicago Board Options Exchange (CBOE) option activity, the put-to-call ratio is the total number of puts traded divided by the number of calls traded on a daily basis. However, there are a variety of put-to-call ratios available, including those that separate equity-only ratios, index-only ratios, and ratios for other exchanges. These particular ratios represent total activity, rather than new purchases of the options. As a result, sentiment can be skewed if many "sell to open" positions are created.

Seasonal pattern: The tendency of the stock market to behave in a certain manner on specific days (or series of days). Examples of seasonal patterns include bullish phases from November 1 through the third trading day in May, or the two trading days immediately prior to an exchange holiday. Other more lightly followed trends include skirt lengths, the Super Bowl indicator, and sports-related results.

Selling climax: A volume surge at a bottom reversal—this is a bullish signal.

Sentiment analysis: Evaluation of the prevailing crowd psychology, which many believe to move markets.

Sentiment indicator: A tool used to gauge the prevailing crowd psychology. Sentiment indicators include put-to-call ratios, sentiment indexes, and mutual fund data reports.

Short interest: Short interest is calculated each month by the exchanges and indicates how many shares are being shorted. The short interest ratio indicates how many days it would take of normal volume for all the short shares to be covered. The higher the number, the more the stock will move to the upside when the shorts start to cover.

Size effect: An anomaly that compares performance of stocks in terms of market capitalization. Small caps tend to outperform large caps over the long haul—since 1991, the Russell 2000 Small Cap Index ($RUT) is up 450 percent, compare to a 235 percent gain for the large-cap S&P 500 Index ($SPX).

Smart money: Groups of investors that have a history of accurately timing the market are sometimes referred to as smart money. They are generally large investors that take big positions and include commercial hedgers and OEX traders.

Titanic Syndrome: A market crash signal triggered when the Dow Jones Industrial Average either hits a new high for the year or rallies 400 points, but the number of new lows on the NYSE outnumbers the new highs within seven days of the Dow's high. This signal was created more than 40 years ago and is credited to Bill Omaha.

TRIN (also Arms Index): The TRIN, also referred to as the Arms Index for its developer, Dick Arms, measures buying and selling pressure through the use of both advancing and declining statistics, along with volume statistics. The ratio calculation is as follows:

$$\text{TRIN} = \frac{(\text{Volume for decliners/\# Decliners})}{(\text{Volume for advancers/\# Advancers})}$$

Up volume: The volume of the issues on the stock exchange that are moving higher in price.

Value Line enigma: Value Line is well known for its quantitative analysis research used to rank stocks based on earnings momentum, technical indicators, and risk. Several academic studies have analyzed the returns, and the results have supported Value Line's ability to outperform the broad market, contrary to efficient market theory.

Volume: The total number of shares associated with a specific stock or market. Also known as *turnover*, it reflects the number of shares bought or sold relative to a specific security over a specific time frame. It can be applied to two different situations—on an index or security basis and on an exchange basis.

Sector Trading

SUMMARY

Chapter 11 is a key part of *The Index Trading Course*. Although basic index and strategy information was required prior to this point, sector trading is at the heart of any trader who picks up this book. As traders, we want to understand what is moving various stock groups and to capitalize on those moves. Monitoring sector rotation and the economic conditions that favor one group over another are some of the methods covered here.

In order to formulate a rational sector strategy, a trader needs to understand how sectors move relative to broad indexes and to one another. The tendency for one group to lead another group upward or for two securities to be well correlated can change, as with any other market relationship. There are no absolutes when it comes to the markets. However, recognizing that these relationships exist, constructing strategies that are consistent with them, and managing risk increases the chances of trading profitability.

Along with sectors previously discussed in the book, we introduce different bond instruments in Chapter 11. This group fits in nicely when one considers how these investments impact the flow of money into and out of other securities. In addition, long-standing relationships exist between stocks and bonds.

QUESTIONS AND EXERCISES

1. A challenge of sector rotation is the trader's ability to _____.
    A. Time the market.
    B. Find index proxies to trade.
    C. Be approved by a broker for sector trading.
    D. Pay the commissions.

2. Which sector is generally less impacted by interest rates?
    A. Banks.
    B. Utilities.
    C. Consumer discretionary.
    D. Consumer staples.

3. Collectively, the nine Select Sector SPDRs hold the _____ stocks.
    A. 100 NASDAQ 100.
    B. 30 Dow Industrial Average.
    C. 500 S&P 500.
    D. 100 S&P 100.

4. True or false: During periods of strong group rotation, the market cannot trade flat since specific sectors trend higher or lower.

5. Combined analysis blends all but the following forms of analysis:
    A. Fundamental.
    B. Speculative.
    C. Sentiment.
    D. Technical.

6. Semiconductor stocks _____ tend to lead other technology stocks.
    A. Do.
    B. Do not.

7. Match the debt type with its description by placing the proper number in the space provided.

   A. T-Note   _____   1. Does not make interest payments,

   B. Convertible bond   is moderately discounted.

   C. Zero coupon bond   _____   2. Is deeply discounted.

   D. T-Bill   _____   3. U.S.-issued bond maturing in 1 to

   E. T-Bond   10 years.

              _____   4. U.S.-issued bond maturing in more

                  than 10 years.

              _____   5. Bond that can be turned into shares

                  of stock.

8. True or false: Since sector rotation prompts large moves, it is reasonable to trade less liquid sector products.

9. True or false: REITs are investment vehicles similar to mutual funds with shares that receive the end-of-the-day net asset value (NAV) when purchased.

10. The yield curve is said to be inverted when _____ yields are higher than _____ yields.

    A. Short-term / long-term.

    B. Long-term / short-term.

    C. Corporate / government.

    D. Government / corporate.

11. Utility stocks experience _____ competition from bonds when rates rise.

    A. Less.

    B. More.

    C. Unpredictable.

    D. No.

12. True or false: Certain sector volatilities can change over time.

13. Credit risk from _____ is high.
    A. Zero coupon bonds.
    B. Corporate high-grade bonds.
    C. Long-term Treasury bonds.
    D. Junk bonds.

14. Interest rate risk from _____ is high.
    A. Treasury short-term notes.
    B. Corporate convertible bonds.
    C. Long-term Treasury bonds.
    D. Ginnie Mae (GNMA).

15. True or false: The Five Year Note Index ($FVX), the Ten Year Note Index ($TNX), and the Thirty Year Bond Index ($TYX) are used to monitor changes in interest rates.

16. Which is *not* one of the six basic principles of Dow theory?
    A. The averages discount everything.
    B. The Dow Transports should confirm the Dow Industrials.
    C. Volume should expand in the direction of the trend.
    D. An inverted yield curve warns of an unhealthy economy.

17. True or false: Pairs trading is best performed with uncorrelated securities.

MEDIA ASSIGNMENT

The media assignment for this chapter requires you to access the Internet so you can visually observe correlations between different sectors and stocks. This will be accomplished by reviewing various charts from a source that allows you to overlay one or more securities on one chart. If you do not have access to such a charting package, access the free charts on Optionetics.com.

Begin by reviewing the following combinations on weekly or three-year charts: major indexes with sector indexes or sector ETFs, pairs of sector indexes or ETFs, ETFs and component stocks, and finally, stocks within the same sector. The primary goal of this assignment is to really see how different sectors and stocks move in relation to one another. Weekly charts are used so that the longer-term relationships are viewed rather than shorter-term ones. When reviewing the charts, keep in mind that any indicators or tools added to the chart are based on the original security displayed, not the comparison security.

Based on the charts you viewed, did any of them display price dynamics to support the underlying theory for pairs trading?

VOCABULARY LIST

British Thermal Unit (BTU)

Convertible bond

Coupon

DRAM

Economic cycle

GNMA

Group rotation

Junk bond

Pair trade

Pairs trading

Real estate investment trust (REIT)

Sector rotation

Spot price

Treasury Bill (T-Bill)

Treasury Bond (T-Bond)

Treasury Note (T-Note)

Yield curve

SOLUTIONS

1. A challenge of sector rotation is the trader's ability to _____.

   Answer: A—Time the market.

   Discussion: Sector rotation is sometimes shunned because it is a form of market timing. However, recent research in this area of trading suggests there are potential benefits from properly executed sector rotation strategies, thus countering the EMT argument.

2. Which sector is generally less impacted by interest rates?

   Answer: B—Consumer staples.

   Discussion: The consumer staples sector includes "necessary" items and is generally less impacted by rising rates or an economic slowdown. When short-term rates rise relative to long-term rates, profits can suffer since this represents the difference between the banks' borrowing and their lending to others. Utilities face stiffer competition from interest-based securities, and money may also shift out of stable, blue chip sectors such as pharmaceuticals.

3. Collectively, the nine Select Sector SPDRs hold the _____ stocks.

   Answer: C—500 S&P 500.

   Discussion: The Select Sector SPDRs include those covering financials, information technology, health care, consumer discretionary, industrials, consumer staples, energy, basic materials, and utilities sectors. Combined, these ETFs account for all S&P 500 stocks.

4. True or false: During periods of strong group rotation, the market cannot trade flat since specific sectors trend higher or lower.

   Answer: False.

   Discussion: Sector rotation results in one sector falling while another rises as money moves out of one sector and into another. Although the market as a whole may rise or decline during these periods, there are also times when the movement in one sector acts counter to the other, resulting in flat trading for the market.

5. Combined analysis blends all but the following forms of analysis:

   Answer: B—Speculative.

   Discussion: Fundamental, technical, and sentiment are all forms of analysis discussed in this text. A trader can focus on one discipline or blend them together to select sectors to trade, create strategies, and make entry and exit decisions. "Speculative analysis" suggests risky trading that is not recommended.

6. Semiconductor stocks _____ tend to lead other technology stocks.

   Answer: A—Do.

   Discussion: Although there will exist times when different market relationships fail or change, there have been extended periods when semiconductors lead technology in general. The fundamental explanation of such a dynamic is that chip orders are initiated by increased demand for technology products. However, impact from increased orders reaches semiconductor share prices first, followed by increases in tech shares as their sales increase.

7. Match the debt type with its description by placing the proper number in the space provided.

   Answer:

   A. T-Note—3. U.S.-issued bond maturing in 1 to 10 years.
   B. Convertible bond—5. Bond that can be turned into shares of stock.
   C. Zero coupon bond—2. Is deeply discounted.
   D. T-Bill—1. Does not make interest payments, is moderately discounted.
   E. T-Bond—4. U.S.-issued bond maturing in more than 10 years.

8. True or false: Since sector rotation prompts large moves, it is reasonable to trade less liquid sector products.

   Answer: False.

   Discussion: Given the very wide range of liquid products available to sector traders, there is no reason to trade illiquid contracts unless there is a very unique investor situation.

9. True or false: REITs are investment vehicles similar to mutual funds with shares that receive the end-of-the-day net asset value (NAV) when purchased.

   Answer: False.

   Discussion: By definition, REITs are investment vehicles with shares listed for trading on the U.S. stock exchanges. Each trust invests in a different type of real estate property. There is also an ETF that tracks the Cohen & Steers Realty Majors Index Fund, which holds a basket of real estate investment trusts (REITs). As with other ETFs, this ETF is also traded throughout the day on an exchange.

10. The yield curve is said to be inverted when _____ yields are higher than _____ yields.

    Answer: A—Short-term / long-term.

    Discussion: Long-term Treasuries have higher interest rate risk and therefore generally have higher yields—the increased yield is necessary to entice investors to buy the more risky bonds. Interest rate risk is the risk that rates will increase, making existing bonds less valuable. When short-term rates increase, the curve constructed using Treasury yields inverts (has a negative slope), which signals near-term concerns about the economy.

11. Utility stocks experience _____ competition from bonds when rates rise.

    Answer: B—More.

    Discussion: Utility shares typically offer high dividends and therefore compete with interest-bearing instruments. As yields rise, bonds become more appealing because investors can earn similar interest while benefiting from a higher safety of principal—there is no stock market risk for bonds. This creates more competition for utility stocks.

12. True or false: Certain sector volatilities can change over time.

    Answer: True.

    Discussion: Prior to deregulation, the utility sector was very stable. However, changes in the way the sector as a whole conducts business have changed this stability. Utility firms are now more affected by supply and demand issues, similar to other stocks. Sector volatility was significantly impacted as a result of these changes. Similarly, a highly volatile sector could face reduced volatility if the government stepped in to regulate supply-demand issues or some other similar structural change occurred.

13. Credit risk from _____ is high.

    Answer: D—Junk bonds.

    Discussion: Credit risk is a safety-of-principal risk that is affected by a company's ability to pay its debts. Federal and high grade (investment grade) bonds are deemed to have low credit risk due to the taxing authority of the government and financial strength of corporations, respectively.

14. Interest rate risk from _____ is high.

    Answer: C— Long-term Treasury bonds.

    Discussion: Interest rate risk is the risk associated with bond values decreasing as rates increase. The longer term to maturity for a bond, the longer it is subject to such risk. This translates to a relatively higher interest rate risk for longer-term bonds, even Treasuries.

15. True or false: The Five Year Note Index ($FVX), the Ten Year Note Index ($TNX), and the Thirty Year Bond Index ($TYX) are used to monitor changes in interest rates.

    Answer: True.

    Discussion: These indexes actually represent the current rates afforded to various government bonds. For example, the Ten Year Note Index reflects the current rate on the benchmark Ten Year Treasury Note multiplied by a factor of 10. So, if the current yield on the Ten Year is 4.4 percent, the TNX will be trading at 44.00. In the same manner, the FVX trades the Five Year Note and the TNX tracks the Thirty Year Bond.

16. Which is *not* one of the six basic principles of Dow theory?

    Answer: D—An inverted yield curve warns of an unhealthy economy.

    Discussion: Although an inverted yield curve does signal a warning to traders of a potentially unhealthy economy, it is not one of the tenets included in Dow's market theories and observations.

17. True or false: Pairs trading is best performed with uncorrelated securities.

    Answer: False.

    Discussion: Pairs trading relies on temporary changes in movement for two securities that are typically highly correlated. The theory behind such a strategy is that the relationship will return to normal as the correlation value reverts to its mean. Pairs traders seek to capture the move back to normalcy.

MEDIA ASSIGNMENT

The media assignment for this chapter requires the reader to access the Internet to visually observe correlations between different sectors and stocks. This is accomplished by reviewing various charts with overlay capabilities. The charting portion of the Optionetics web site has such features and can be accessed by entering a symbol on the home page and selecting "Charting," then "GO." Since the initial focus was on major indexes, we first queried the chart for $NDX, the NASDAQ 100 Index. We decided to use semiconductor stocks as a comparison sector and added SMH, the semiconductor ETF, as an overlay to the NDX chart. In order to best observe the longer-term trend, the three-year, "large" chart setting was selected and is displayed in Figure 11.1.

Once this chart is put in black and white format, it is difficult to discern one security from the other. The SMH is the more volatile of the two and forms a peak in January 2004. This same line retraces to approximately 15 percent in July of the same year. The movement in the index and ETF is very similar; however, clearly there were some other NDX 100

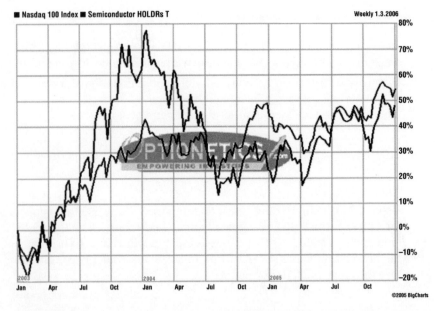

FIGURE 11.1   NDX Weekly Chart with SMH Overlay (*Source:* www.Optionetics .com)

components dampening the rise in this index from July through December 2003. Whether these components were part of a specific technology sector requires further investigation.

Volatility continues in SMH as it declines more severely into July 2004, and the ETF finally begins to catch up to the NDX on a relative basis in mid-2005. The movement in the last year appears to be more consistent with the normal relationship between the two. Confirming this would require a review of a longer-term chart. The leading nature of semiconductors is more apparent after January 2004, when peaks and troughs for the ETF occurred ever so slightly before the NDX.

When considering a pairs trade opportunity, we need to switch from a chart that includes the $NDX to one that includes QQQQ since an index cannot be traded directly. Figure 11.2 is very similar to the previous one, but includes QQQQ as the base chart with SMH overlaid. The other settings remain the same.

Based on the QQQQ-SMH chart, it does appear that a pairs trading approach is rational. During the period from mid-2003 through the end of that year, SMH was accelerating upward more quickly than QQQQ. As the

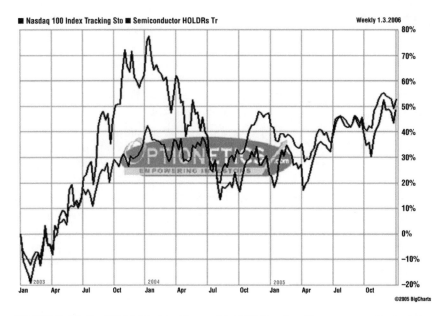

FIGURE 11.2 QQQQ Weekly Chart with SMH Overlay (*Source:* www.Optionetics .com)

two diverged, a pairs trading opportunity was beginning to unfold. As mentioned in Chapter 11, however, this skew in the relationship was able to persist for an extended period and would have proven to be a difficult position to sustain if it had been established in early October. That is why risk management must always be a component of any trade strategy. A strategist using additional tools to monitor the SMH move based on its underlying breadth may have been able to better time a trade for this pair of securities.

VOCABULARY DEFINITIONS

British Thermal Unit (BTU): An output measurement for the natural gas industry that is used for fundamental analysis.

Convertible bond: A form of debt issued by a company that also gives the holder the right to convert the debt instrument to shares of stock in the company. The specific conversion details are predetermined, and this feature will generally increase the value of the bond, resulting in a lower yield.

Coupon: The interest rate the issuer promises to pay over the lifetime of a debt security.

DRAM: Dynamic random access memory (DRAM) chips are the most common type of semiconductor memory chips and are used in devices like computers, MP3 players, and digital cameras. They have become actively traded in the spot market like commodities.

Economic cycle: The tendency for the economy to experience periods of growth and periods of decline, as reflected by the gross domestic product (GDP) statistics. The average cycle is approximately 5.5 years from peak to trough and returning to the peak.

GNMA: "Ginnie Mae," the Government National Mortgage Association, a quasi-governmental entity that issues debt based on pools of mortgages. Since the full taxing authority of the U.S. government does not guarantee the debt, GNMA bond rates are higher than those for Treasuries. However, the bonds are guaranteed by the entity itself and are generally deemed safer than corporate bonds and will therefore offer a lower yield than such instruments.

Group rotation: See *sector rotation*.

Junk bond: A high-risk, below-investment-grade corporate bond.

Pair trade: A market neutral strategy that attempts to profit from the fact that certain stocks tend to exhibit a high degree of co-movement over the long term.

Pairs trading: A strategy that uses two securities with high correlations that have recently become less correlated. When the usual relationship between the two securities changes, it is assumed that they will eventually return to their historical correlation. To capitalize on this temporary change, the pairs trader will go long one security (temporarily lower in price) and short the other (temporarily higher in price) until the normal relationship between the two is restored.

Real estate investment trust (REIT): A trust that invests in real estate, with shares that trade on an exchange like stock. These entities often specialize in certain types of real estate, such as shopping malls, apartments, or office buildings.

Sector rotation (or group rotation): The process of moving money to different areas of the market in anticipation of one sector performing better than the other.

Spot price: The current delivery price for a specific commodity or underlying index. It serves as the pricing basis for futures contracts.

Treasury Bill (T-Bill): Debt issued by the U.S. Treasury Department that is backed by the U.S. government's full taxing authority is referred to as a Treasury. A T-Bill is debt that matures one year or less after the date it is issued.

Treasury Bond (T-Bond): Debt issued by the U.S. Treasury Department, backed by the U.S. government's full taxing authority, that matures more than 10 years after it is issued (generally up to 30 years).

Treasury Note (T-Note): Debt issued by the U.S. Treasury Department, backed by the U.S. government's full taxing authority, that matures between 1 and 10 years after it is issued.

Yield curve: A curve constructed from Treasury debt available that includes the most recently issued debt ("on the run") to debt that has already been issued ("off the run"). It includes the shortest-term through the longest-term issues available, with longer-term debt typically yielding a higher rate, thus causing an upward-sloped curve. When short-term yields are higher, it is referred to as an *inverted yield curve.*

Tracking and Trading Volatility

SUMMARY

While all traders need to understand volatility for the securities they trade, option traders need to deepen this understanding since volatility is directly related to the value of the option. There are many different types and terms for volatility, including implied, historical, and statistical. To maximize the benefits of options trading, strategists should recognize what drives implied volatility and the conditions that favor certain trades over others.

Volatility can be visualized with different chart tools or by tracking various levels of volatility on a regular basis. Certain pricing models will help the trader determine the value of implied volatility; however, by itself, this one number has limited use. By comparing the current implied volatility to statistical volatility and previous levels of implied volatility, the trader has a much better ability to select appropriate strategies.

Chapter 12 presents a concise explanation of measurements of stock and option volatility, as well as the means to monitor them. It discusses the types of strategies a trader should consider given certain volatility environments and wraps up the topic with a look at portfolio and position hedging.

QUESTIONS AND EXERCISES

1. When the volatility of the underlying security is expected to be high going forward, option premiums should be _____.

   A. Stable.

   B. Low.

   C. Depends on *rho*.

   D. High.

2. The VIX is an index based on the current prices of the _____ options.

   A. S&P 100.

   B. S&P 500.

   C. NASDAQ 100.

   D. Russell 1000.

3. When a model is used to compute the volatility priced into an option premium, it is referred to as _____ volatility.

   A. Modeled.

   B. Theoretical.

   C. Implied.

   D. Statistical.

4. True or false: Bollinger Bands make use of both moving averages and standard deviations to provide contracting and expanding price ranges.

5. The higher the standard deviation, the _____ stock prices are dispersed.

   A. More.

   B. Less.

   C. Additional information is required.

6. What condition below *does not* describe or include a reason for an increase in the implied volatility (IV) calculation?
    A. Increased demand in options contracts.
    B. Recently increased statistical volatility.
    C. Pending earnings report.
    D. Increased supply in options contracts.

7. It is not uncommon to find reverse skews in the _____ since options with a lower strike price have higher implied volatility than those with higher strike prices.
    A. Cash index market.
    B. Bull market.
    C. Bear market.
    D. Not applicable—reverse skews rarely exist.

8. True or false: If IV is considerably lower than its historical volatility, it is a sign that the market is pricing in or bracing for an increase in volatility going forward.

9. True or false: When looking at the implied volatility (IV), the options strategist will want to understand both the IV and statistical volatility (SV) over time and compare the two.

10. A good index for QQQQ traders to watch is the _____ constructed and reported by AMEX.
    A. Revised VIX.
    B. QQQQ Volatility Index (QQV).
    C. Former VIX (VXO).
    D. QQQQ Deviation Index (STDEV).

11. If the SPX is trading near the 900 level, one put option will protect a(n) _____ portfolio.
    A. Institutional.
    B. $90,000.
    C. Retail.
    D. $450.

MEDIA ASSIGNMENT

For this media assignment, the reader is encouraged to visit the Optionetics web site, www.optionetics.com, and use the free volatility ranker. The idea is to screen for indexes that have relatively cheap or expensive options based on current levels of implied volatility.

The first step is to type www.optionetics.com into the web browser (this also makes a great home page for traders, incidentally). Next, find the "Options Volatility Ranking" box, about halfway down the page in the right-hand column. There are several choices within that box ("Expensive," "Cheap," "Explosive," "Quiet," and "More").

Click on the "Cheap" button. A list of 50 securities will appear. These stocks or indexes are ones that have relatively low implied volatility (IV). To be more specific, the "cheap" ranking produces a list of options with an IV that is at the lower end of the one-year range. Scroll down the list and identify any indexes. Sometimes there will be many and sometimes very few. If the CBOE Volatility Index ($VIX) is at the lower end of its one-year range, several indexes will appear in the "cheap" list.

The "expensive" list, by contrast, will list the stocks and indexes that have IV in the higher end of the one-year range. Repeat the process and look for indexes that have high implied volatility. If you find an index, click on the symbol and look at the implied volatility chart. If it is "expensive," the IV chart will be trending higher.

Index traders want to continually track the implied volatility of the index options they like to trade. The CBOE Volatility Index provides a quick look at the IV of the S&P 500 Index. However, VIX doesn't always reflect what is happening with other indexes or within specific sectors. The Optionetics ranker can help identify areas of the market where options are becoming cheap (low IV) or expensive (high IV).

VOCABULARY LIST

Expected volatility

Hedge

Historical volatility

Implied volatility (IV)

Partial hedge

Perfect hedge

Price skew

Skew

Standard deviation

Statistical volatility (SV)

Time skew

SOLUTIONS

1. When the volatility of the underlying security is expected to be high going forward, option premiums should be _____.

   Answer: D—High.

   Discussion: On a given day, with the price of the underlying momentarily fixed, gamma, delta, and theta will all remain fixed as well. The only thing that is subject to change with expectations of greater price movement in the underlying (volatility) is implied volatility. As this value increases with expectations, premiums will also increase.

2. The VIX is an index based on the current prices of the _____ options.

   Answer: B—S&P 500.

   Discussion: The VIX was previously based on implied volatility calculations for the S&P 100 Index (the first index that served as an underlying for options). However, in late 2004 the CBOE changed both the underlying and the construction for the VIX. Now it is based on the S&P 500 and has a slightly different means of being calculated. This data has been historically reconstructed for the VIX. Additionally, the original VIX using the S&P 100 remains available as the S&P 100 Volatility Index (VXO) and is updated daily.

3. When a model is used to compute the volatility priced into an option premium, it is referred to as _____ volatility.

   Answer: C—Implied.

   Discussion: Implied volatility is defined as the consensus cost of future volatility as reflected in the options premium and is computed using options pricing models.

4. True or false: Bollinger Bands make use of both moving averages and standard deviations to provide contracting and expanding price ranges.

   Answer: True.

   Discussion: By definition, Bollinger Bands are constructed by creating upper and lower bands on a price chart. The baseline is usually a 20-period simple moving average (SMA) line, with the upper band created by adding two standard deviations to the SMA and the lower band created by subtracting two standard deviations from the SMA.

Based on statistical measurements and the type of data being measured, the expanding and contracting bands capture 95 percent of the price action over the last 20 periods. When prices move beyond the band, a significant change in volatility during this period is occurring.

5. The higher the standard deviation, the _____ stock prices are dispersed.

Answer: A—More.

Discussion: Standard deviation is calculated using an average (mean) measurement for a data set, then evaluating the distance each data point is away from this average. In this way, a single value provides the statistician with information about potentially large pools of data, relative to the average value. The greater the standard deviation, the more dispersed or farther away data appears from the average of the set.

6. What condition below *does not* describe or include a reason for an increase in the implied volatility (IV) calculation?

Answer: D—Increased supply in options contracts.

Discussion: Since IV reflects future expected movement from the underlying, it will increase when the underlying has experienced more price movement in the recent past (increased SV) or if there is uncertainty in the near future (earnings report). In addition, IV can be thought of as the missing piece in options pricing and can be somewhat inappropriately affected by contract supply and demand issues. As more demand enters the market, prices will go up, resulting in increased IV calculations. When supply enters the market, prices will naturally go down, resulting in decreased IV calculations.

7. It is not uncommon to find reverse skews in the _____ since options with a lower strike price have higher implied volatility than those with higher strike prices.

Answer: A—Cash index market.

Discussion: Since the 1987 stock market crash, options with a lower strike price have higher implied volatility than those with higher strike prices. Lower-strike puts become more expensive as the potential for a significant drop (crash) remains present in the minds of traders. On the other side of the directional bet, prices tend to increase over the long run. This reverse price skew is not uncommon in the cash index market and is not dependent on market direction (bullish or bearish).

8. True or false: If IV is considerably lower than its historical volatility, it is a sign that the market is pricing in or bracing for an increase in volatility going forward.

Answer: False.

Discussion: When IV is low, the price of the option is relatively low since IV represents one pricing component. Such an occurrence is caused by flat movement in the underlying with no news on the horizon. As concerns about a price shock increase, the chance for an option to move in-the-money (or further in-the-money) increases, raising the price of the option via an increase in IV.

9. True or false: When looking at the implied volatility (IV), the options strategist will want to understand both the IV and statistical volatility (SV) over time and compare the two.

Answer: True.

Discussion: It is not enough merely to obtain a reading for IV; the trader needs to understand where this reading is relative to previous IV readings, as well as past movements in the underlying security as reflected by the SV readings. Certain options analysis packages provide this information in chart form so the comparison is straightforward.

10. A good index for QQQQ traders to watch is the _____ constructed and reported by AMEX.

Answer: B—QQQQ Volatility Index (QQV).

Discussion: The QQQQ Volatility Index is a composite measure of implied volatility on QQQQ options created by the AMEX. It is computed and available throughout the day. The VIX and VXO are volatility measurements for the S&P 500 and S&P 100, respectively, and while helpful are not better measurements than a QQQQ measurement.

11. If the SPX is trading near the 900 level, one put option will protect a(n) _____ portfolio.

Answer: B—$90,000.

Discussion: Since options on the S&P 500 Index are cash-settled and have a multiplier of 100, one 900 put is in-the-money for all movement below 900. Let's assume the S&P 500 moves from 900 to 875, where it closes at expiration. The long 900-strike put holder receives cash settlement of $2,500 [(900 − 875) × 100 = 2,500]. A portfolio based on the

S&P 500 and worth $90,000 when the S&P 500 was 900 has now lost $2,500 in value ($90,000 − $87,500 = $2,500). In such an example the put was a perfect hedge for this portfolio.

MEDIA ASSIGNMENT

In this chapter, the focus is on volatility. There are several ways to measure volatility, including statistical volatility (SV), the average true range (ATR), and implied volatility (IV). To the options trader, all measures are important, but implied volatility is at the top of the list. It tells the strategist not only about the potential volatility of the underlying asset, but also whether the option premiums are cheap or expensive. If IV is low, the options are cheap. When IV is high, they are relatively expensive.

Understanding the trends with respect to implied volatility will help make sense of the changes in the value of the options contract. First, traders want to consider the IV before the position is established. For example, if the strategist buys a put option when IV is at the higher end of its range, the position can lose value in two ways. First, if the underlying asset moves higher, the put option will lose value. In addition, if implied volatility falls, the put option will also lose value. The loss of value related to changes in volatility is known as vega risk.

In fact, many investors use index put options at exactly the wrong time. Remember the adage, "When VIX is high, it's time to buy. When VIX is low, it's time to go." It refers to the fact that, when VIX is high, it is time to buy into the stock market. It is a sign that pessimism has reached an extreme and investors are too bearish. From a contrarian view, this is a time to buy calls, not puts, because the market is likely to move higher. However, when VIX, the market's "fear gauge," is high, index put volume is often on the rise. Investors are buying them to protect their portfolios out of fear or anxiety. Then, when the pessimism begins to dissipate and the market reverses direction and heads higher, those puts in turn lose value due to the move higher in the index and because of the drop in implied volatility. In sum, index traders want to be aware how IV affects their positions and not to become an aggressive buyer when the options are expensive. It is much better to buy options when they are cheap. The free ranker at Optionetics.com can help find examples of each.

VOCABULARY DEFINITIONS

Expected volatility: Also known as implied volatility, expected volatility is a measure of volatility that is computed using options pricing models. These measures of volatility are priced into or embedded into current option prices and reflect consensus expectations about future volatility of the underlying index.

Hedge: A trade that reduces the risk of an existing position and is used primarily in the options and futures markets.

Historical volatility: A measure of past price changes in a stock or index. Historical volatility is a look in the rearview mirror. It can be viewed using OHLC range bars or the average true range and is calculated using statistics.

Implied volatility (IV): The consensus cost of future volatility as reflected in the options premium. It is computed using options pricing models. Although statistical (a.k.a. historical) volatility plays a role in implied volatility, pending news releases, spikes in market activity, and supply and demand can also impact expectations about stock movement, and therefore option prices.

Partial hedge: A partial hedge removes a portion of the risk from a position.

Perfect hedge: A perfect hedge removes all risk from a position. The hedge portion of the position may require adjustment as the base position or portfolio changes in value.

Price skew: An option characteristic where options with different strike prices have different implied volatility.

Skew: A volatility skew describes an option chain characteristic in which different options contracts on the same underlying asset have different levels of implied volatility. Skews may occur between options with different expirations, between similar calls and puts, or between calls and puts with different strike prices.

Standard deviation: The standard deviation is a calculation using mean values from a data set to describe how dispersed the data set is from the expected mean of an entire population. This measurement describes characteristics of the whole data set in relation to an average value for the data set. In terms of stock prices, the standard deviation can be used with averages to provide a range in which price is expected to travel—this chart indicator is referred to as Bollinger Bands.

Statistical volatility (SV): Statistical volatility is the mostly widely used gauge of historical or actual volatility among options traders. It is computed using the closing price of the stock or index over a fixed number of trading days. Mathematically, it is computed as the annualized standard deviation of prices over a period of days. High standard deviations are generally associated with higher-risk, or higher-volatility, investments.

Time skew: An option characteristic where options with different expirations have different implied volatility.

CHAPTER 13

Making Adjustments

SUMMARY

Option traders have the ability to adjust trades, providing them with added flexibility when trading sectors. Unfortunately, added flexibility can also mean added decision making—a difficult task once a position is established. To successfully benefit from adjustments, traders need to have some criteria on which to base their decisions. First and foremost, the result of making an adjustment should *not* be that the trader assumes more risk.

Position adjustment goals include locking in profits by closing part of the trade or using money management to reduce the size of the trade at a predetermined profitability level. The trader can also roll the trade up (higher strike) or out (longer-term option) or add contracts to improve the risk/reward profile. Finally, the original strategy—a delta or gamma neutral trade—may warrant adjustments as the price of the underlying changes.

Chapter 13 provides the reader with additional insight into option Greeks by discussing changes to these measurements during the life of the trade that may necessitate trade adjustment. Another, clearer reason for making an adjustment would be the trader's change of outlook. Both of these factors are addressed through discussion and example.

QUESTIONS AND EXERCISES

1. Option traders may choose to _____ a position through expiration or _____ a position through adjustments.
   A. Actively manage / monitor.
   B. Monitor / actively manage.
   C. Monitor / passively manage.
   D. Passively manage / monitor.

2. A directional vertical spread is a(n) _____ risk and reward position with the extent of the trader's bearishness or bullishness reflected in the strikes.
   A. High.
   B. Adjusted.
   C. Immediate.
   D. Limited.

3. Adjustments attempt to _____ and minimize _____.
   A. Lock in profits / risk.
   B. Fix a losing position / commissions.
   C. Lock in profits / commissions.
   D. Minimize risk / commissions.

4. True or false: One benefit of a delta neutral trade is that it remains directionally neutral throughout the life of the trade, without adjustment.

5. The option Greek that measures the change in the delta with respect to the change in price of the underlying security is _____.
   A. Delta.
   B. Theta.
   C. Gamma.
   D. Vega.

6. A long straddle has gamma risk, which can be profitable when there is _____ in the underlying security.
   A. Stability.
   B. Time remaining.
   C. Movement.
   D. Theta acceleration.

7. Match the term with its definition by placing the proper number in the space provided.
   A. Intrinsic value _____   1. Greater time value.
   B. Extrinsic value _____   2. Peak gamma value.
   C. ATM call option _____   3. Associated with time value.
   D. OTM call option _____   4. Delta > 0.50.
   E. ITM call option _____   5. Associated with ITM value.

8. True or false: The value of gamma peaks when the underlying is trading near the option strike price.

9. True or false: An increase in implied volatility translates to an increase in vega, which is good for the long option holder.

10. A delta neutral, natural long straddle includes a long call and a long put while a delta neutral, synthetic long straddle can include _____ and _____.
    A. 100 long shares / one ATM long put.
    B. 100 long shares / one ATM long call.
    C. 100 long shares / two ATM long puts.
    D. 100 long shares / two ATM long calls.

11. When a trader makes adjustments, which question should *not* be asked in the process?
    A. How much? (How close to lock in profits.)
    B. Where to? (Price projection for strike selection.)
    C. How long? (Time projection for expiration selection.)
    D. When? (When will it go in the direction I need it to go?)

MEDIA ASSIGNMENT

In Chapter 13, the reader is introduced to the concept of *adjustments*. An adjustment is a modification to an existing position. Adjustments can be used to buy more time for the trade, to cut potential losses, to protect profits, or to change the directional bias of the trade. There is no right or wrong way to make an adjustment, but understanding the concept of delta can sometimes simplify and improve the process.

Delta reflects the price change of an options contract for every price change in the underlying asset. For example, a call option with a delta of 0.55 will increase in value by 55 cents for every one-point move higher in the underlying index. Put options have negative deltas. As a result, if the strategist wants to adjust the call option with a delta of 0.55 into a neutral position using a put option, that strategist would buy a put (or puts) with a delta of –0.55. The negative delta from the put will offset the delta of the call, and the position delta will be zero.

There are a number of different ways to find the delta of an options contract. The easiest way is to use an options chain that provides delta information for each contract. These types of chains are available through various brokerage firms and the Optionetics Platinum site. Another way to find the delta of an option is to use an options calculator. This media assignment explores the second approach.

A number of different web sites offer free options calculators. In this exercise, readers can use the one available on the Chicago Board Options Exchange site, www.cboe.com. From the home page, click on "Volatility Optimizer" and find the link to the "Options Calculator." Click on the link, which should bring up the calculator.

Once the calculator is loaded onto the screen, enter the following inputs: "Style" is European; "Price" is 95; "Strike" is 100; "Days to Expiration" is 50; "Volatility" is 20 percent; and the interest rate is 2 percent (or whatever the rate is when you do this exercise). Do not change any of the other boxes. Then click "Calculate." The calculator will compute the theoretical values of puts and calls for an option that has a strike price of 100, 50 days until expiration, and implied volatility of 20 percent. It will also compute the Greeks, including delta.

Using the inputs listed here, the delta for the hypothetical call option is 0.27 and the delta of the put is –0.73. Therefore, the call option will increase in value by $0.27 and the put will lose $0.73 for every one-point move higher in the underlying index. The reader should now be able to compute the delta and other Greeks for any options contract.

VOCABULARY LIST

Adjustment	Intrinsic value
Delta	Long natural straddle
Delta neutral	Long synthetic straddle
Extrinsic value	Theta
Gamma	Theta-wrecking
Gamma scalping	Variable delta

SOLUTIONS

1. Option traders may choose to _____ a position through expiration or _____ a position through adjustments.

   Answer: B—Monitor / actively manage.

   Discussion: Monitoring a position includes being aware of the risk and stop levels needed to properly execute a trade. An options trader can allow his or her position to remain intact through expiration, or may choose to make adjustments along the way. Such adjustments are intended to realize gains or reduce risk.

2. A directional vertical spread is a(n) _____ risk and reward position with the extent of the trader's bearishness or bullishness reflected in the strikes.

   Answer: D—Limited.

   Discussion: Directional vertical spreads use calls or puts with the same expiration dates in spreads that have a 1:1 ratio of short calls (puts) to long calls (puts). As a result, any risk created by the short position is protected to some extent by the long position, and the position represents limited risk. The actual degree of risk is reflected by the difference in strike prices or the original debit, depending on the type of spread (credit or debit). Keep in mind that limited risk can still be high risk, which is why it is beneficial to look at the risk/reward ratio as well.

3. Adjustments attempt to _____ and minimize _____.

   Answer: A—Lock in profits / risk.

   Discussion: Option traders adjust position to lock in profits and minimize risk. With delta neutral or gamma neutral trades, they may also wish to make changes to keep the original strategy on track. In no instance should a trade be adjusted to assume more risk because the trader's original premise or assessment proved incorrect. Adjusting is not a method to postpone losses.

4. True or false: One benefit of a delta neutral trade is that it remains directionally neutral throughout the life of the trade, without adjustment.

   Answer: False.

   Discussion: Delta changes as the price of the underlying changes relative to the option strike price (see *delta variable* in definitions). Deltas are less than +0.50 for out-of-the-money call options, approaching +0.50 as the underlying price approaches the strike price, greater than +0.50 as the option moves in-the-money, and +1.0 as the option moves deep in-the-money. Deltas for puts act similarly but in reverse, with deltas moving from 0 to −1.0.

5. The option Greek that measures the change in the delta with respect to the change in price of the underlying security is _____.

   Answer: C—Gamma.

   Discussion: By definition, gamma is the option Greek used to measure the change in the delta of an option with respect to the change in price of the underlying security.

6. A long straddle has gamma risk, which can be profitable when there is _____ in the underlying security.

   Answer: C—Movement.

   Discussion: As with the other option Greeks, gamma is dynamic rather than static, particularly for options that are not deep ITM or OTM, such as a straddle. The gamma factor associated with this type of position has changed a delta neutral position to one that shows directional risk characteristics. For instance, if the underlying instrument moves dramatically higher in price, although the number of contracts on the straddle hasn't changed, our positive deltas increase. The long calls' deltas move from approximately +50 when the position was established, to possibly a delta near +100, if the move is severe enough. Simultaneously, the puts move from a –50 delta to one that is much lower and possibly approaching zero.

7. Match the term with its definition by placing the proper number in the space provided.

   Answer:

   A. Intrinsic value—5. Associated with ITM value.

   B. Extrinsic value—3. Associated with time value.

   C. ATM call option—2. Peak gamma value.

   D. OTM call option—1. Greater time value.

   E. ITM call option—4. Delta > 0.50.

8. True or false: The value of gamma peaks when the underlying is trading near the option strike price.

   Answer: True.

   Discussion: Gamma has the biggest impact on delta as the price of the underlying moves toward the strike price. As price moves above or below the strike price, gamma decreases, creating less of a change in delta. A call option will continue to increase in value as price increases, but at a decreasing rate. If the price of the underlying instead decreases from the strike, the value of the call option will also decrease at a decreasing rate. This is the impact from gamma.

9. True or false: An increase in implied volatility translates to an increase in vega, which is good for the long option holder.

   Answer: True.

   Discussion: Vega is the option Greek that measures the change in the price of an option with respect to its change in volatility—specifically its implied volatility, which represents future expectations. Although statistical (historical) volatility plays a role in implied volatility, pending news releases, spikes in market activity, and supply and demand can also impact expectations about stock movement, and therefore option prices. A long contract holder owns premium and benefits when vega increases, thus increasing the value of the option.

10. A delta neutral, natural long straddle includes a long call and a long put while a delta neutral, synthetic long straddle can include _____ and _____.

    Answer: C—100 long shares / two ATM long puts.

    Discussion: Each share of stock represents +1 delta, so 100 long shares of stock represents +100 deltas. Since one ATM put has a delta of –50, two puts are needed to create a delta neutral (i.e., delta equal to zero) position: $[100 + 2(-50)] = 100 - 100 = 0$.

11. When a trader makes adjustments, which question should *not* be asked in the process?

    Answer: D—When? (When will it go in the direction I need it to go?)

    Discussion: While the question is one we will inevitably ask ourselves when a trade is moving counter to our expectations, it is not one we should seek an answer to as part of the adjustment process. It is one that is more consistent with hoping for a change. In the event this is occurring, we need to simply manage our risk. The other questions—how much, where to, and how long—are more consistent with strategy-based assessments.

MEDIA ASSIGNMENT

Adjustments can be used in a variety of ways, and sometimes the strategist will want to consider the overall delta of the position before making changes. There are several different ways to find the delta of each options contract. In this media assignment, readers are encouraged to go to the CBOE web site and use the free options calculator in order to compute the delta of a put and a call. For the inputs, we used European Style, a price of 95, a strike of 100, 50 days to expiration, 20 percent volatility, and an interest rate of 2 percent (use whatever the current rate is).

After calculating the theoretical value of a put and a call using these inputs, we found that the delta for the hypothetical call option is 0.27 and the delta of the put is –0.73. Therefore, the call option will increase in value by $0.27 and the put will lose $0.73 for every one-point move higher in the underlying index.

From there, the strategist can change the inputs in order to see how changes in the price of the underlying asset, the time left until expiration, and implied volatility affect delta. Notice first that the out-of-the-money call has a lower delta than the in-the-money put. This will always be the case. Therefore, if the price variable is changed to 105, the call will have a higher delta than the put. If the price is 100, both will have roughly equal deltas.

Notice what happens to the delta of the call if the price is changed from 100 to 101. The delta increases from 0.53 to 0.58. A change in delta due to a change in the price of the index is known as the gamma. In this case, the gamma equals 0.05 because the delta increased by that amount when the index moved one point higher (0.58 – 0.53 = 0.05). Both the delta and the gamma will change as the price of the underlying asset moves higher or lower.

Meanwhile, changing the days until expiration will also affect the Greeks. For instance, if this number is changed to 20 days from 50 days, the delta of both the puts and the calls will increase, which is another way of saying that the options become more sensitive to changes in the underlying asset as expiration approaches. Changes in implied volatility will also affect delta. As an example, changing volatility from 20 percent to 10 percent results in lower deltas while changing it to 30 percent results in higher deltas. In sum, changes in implied volatility can also affect deltas, and this should be taken into consideration when dealing with index options, especially when implied volatility is high and expected to come down.

Options calculators, like the one used in this example, can help traders get a better feel for what is happening with their options contracts and therefore make better adjustments. Delta is an important factor in that process. However, deltas are always changing. Hopefully, this exercise helps readers see how changes in the price of the underlying index, the days left until expiration, and implied volatility can all impact delta. Importantly, not all successful traders know and understand adjustments and Greeks. Nevertheless, understanding these concepts can come in handy when a strategist wants to protect a position or to modify a position that has gone awry.

VOCABULARY DEFINITIONS

Adjustment: The term used to describe changes made to an option position in order to lock in profits and minimize risk. This strategy approach addresses delta or gamma changes when seeking a neutral position or may address changes in the trader's outlook as the underlying moves.

Delta: The option Greek used to measure the change in the price of an option relative to the change in price of the underlying security.

Delta neutral: A position that is constructed in such a way that the net delta of all components is equal to zero—this position is relatively insensitive to the price movement of underlying instruments.

Extrinsic value: The time value for an option premium is known as the extrinsic value. It can also be thought of as the premium amounts above and beyond the intrinsic value.

Call option extrinsic value = Call strike price + Call option price – Stock price

Put option extrinsic value = Stock price + Put option price – Put strike price

Gamma: The option Greek used to measure the change in the delta of an option with respect to the change in price of the underlying security.

Gamma scalping: The adjustment to the delta to get the trader back to a directionally neutral position is called *flattening out* or gamma scalping.

Intrinsic value: The difference between the strike price and the underlying asset's price. The premium value associated with the extent of being in-the-money is the intrinsic value.

Call option intrinsic value = Price of the underlying – Call strike price

Put option intrinsic value = Put strike price – Price of the underlying

Long natural straddle: An option position that is constructed with a long put and a long call (1:1) that have the same strike prices and expiration dates. The strategist expects a significant move in the price of the underlying, either upward or downward.

Long synthetic straddle: A synthetic straddle uses shares (or futures) along with options to replicate a natural straddle position. A delta neutral synthetic straddle can by created by purchasing 100 SPY shares and two SPY puts with deltas of –0.5: Net delta = 1 + 2(–0.5) = 0.

Theta: The option Greek used to measure the change in the price of an option with respect to a change in its time to expiration (time value).

Theta-wrecking: The final 30 days of a contract's life, which experiences accelerated time decay, is referred to as a theta-wrecking period.

Variable delta: Changes in option value reflect changes in the underlying Greeks, including most directly delta. The characteristic for call delta values to move from 0 to 1 and put delta values to move from 0 to –1 is referred to as a variable delta.

CHAPTER 14

Risk Management

SUMMARY

No trading book can be written without a discussion of risk management—it is a key component of any strategy for new and experienced traders alike. Discussion of the general topic of risk management at minimum incorporates specific trade management techniques aimed at setting maximum loss amounts. Other considerations include trade sizing and profit taking.

Risk management may also entail all of the financial steps prior to establishing a trade, in an effort to reduce stress. Not only do traders wish to use proper amounts for each trade; they also need to be sure they have the proper allocations for longer-term investments and trading. Moving up to the biggest view possible, traders should have a sound personal financial plan in place so they are not dictating what the market should give them, but rather look to take what the market is offering them.

Chapter 14 includes brief coverage of the bigger picture, and then moves toward more traditional risk management considerations that include trade management.

QUESTIONS AND EXERCISES

1. _____ refers to the amount of capital a trader wishes to commit to a specific market.
   A. Distribution.
   B. Circulation.
   C. Allocation.
   D. Commitment of traders.

2. When investors or traders allocate funds across and within asset classes, they are said to have _____ their holdings.
   A. Distributed.
   B. Diversified.
   C. Mitigated.
   D. Increased.

3. A relative strength comparison line is a ratio that is constructed by dividing the _____ by the _____.
   A. Average up days / average down days.
   B. S&P 500 stocks / S&P 100 stocks.
   C. Broader benchmark / security or index being analyzed.
   D. Security or index being analyzed / broader benchmark.

4. True or false: A rising relative strength line indicates that the stock being analyzed is increasing in value.

5. A(n) _____ provides the investor with general allocation guidelines while the markets themselves will help dictate how assets are ultimately diversified.
   A. Allocation range.
   B. Assessment plan.
   C. Financial planner's advice.
   D. Roulette wheel.

6. One approach to determining share size for a trade is using a maximum trade allocation value and dividing it by the _____, providing there is a rational maximum risk point for the trade.

A. Projected security price.

B. Current security price.

C. Stop-loss point.

D. Market spread.

7. A portfolio is generally deemed riskier if it holds _____ asset(s) compared to _____ asset(s) that are not perfectly positively correlated.

A. 3 / 1.

B. Cash / stock.

C. 1 / 3.

D. Many / few.

8. True or false: When traders diversify their strategies, they minimize their need to be right.

MEDIA ASSIGNMENT

Chapter 14 deals with risk management, which is ultimately a decision that each individual must consider on his own. Nobody can claim to know how much risk an individual trader should take. Risk tolerance is a personal decision. Therefore, it is somewhat difficult to find a media assignment that can be applied universally to all readers.

However, two important elements of risk management are diversification and asset allocation. Diversification simply means to spread one's risks across different securities or types of securities. It's a fancy way of saying don't put all your eggs in one basket. Asset allocation is a term used to describe investing in different groups of securities: stocks, bonds, gold, and so on.

In this exercise, the reader will track the performance of more than one market in order to see how a diversified portfolio will perform differently from a portfolio that is heavily weighted toward one asset group. To do so, create two hypothetical portfolios. Assume that each portfolio has a total of $30,000 in cash. Under one scenario, the investor buys $30,000 worth of NASDAQ QQQQ shares. To determine the share amount, divide $30,000 by the current price of the QQQQ. Under the other scenario, the investor purchases $10,000 of QQQQ shares, $10,000 of the iShares Long-Term Bond

Fund (TLT), and $10,000 of the streetTracks Gold Fund (GLD). To compute the share amounts, divide $10,000 by the current share price for each fund.

Now, using a spreadsheet, track the changes on a weekly or monthly basis to see how the volatility and value of each portfolio changes over time. The goal is to see how diversifying across different markets can change the risk/reward of a long-term investment strategy. See the discussion for a historical example.

VOCABULARY LIST

Asset class	Overlay chart
Diversification	Relative strength line
Drawdown	Risk management
Good till canceled (GTC)	Risk tolerance
Money management	Stop-loss
Money market	

SOLUTIONS

1. _____ refers to the amount of capital a trader wishes to commit to a specific market.

   Answer: C—Allocation.

   Discussion: By definition the term used to describe the amount of capital committed to a specific market, sector, security, or strategy is referred to as allocation.

2. When investors or traders allocate funds across and within asset classes, they are said to have _____ their holdings.

   Answer: B—Diversified.

   Discussion: By definition, diversification refers to investing or trading within different assets and/or groups. This is done to minimize the impact of one underperforming market or one security having a negative impact on the assets as a whole. By diversifying, an investor avoids needing to time the markets and holds securities that will dampen the impact of downward price movements from other securities.

3. A relative strength comparison line is a ratio that is constructed by dividing the _____ by the _____.

   Answer: D—Security or index being analyzed / broader benchmark.

   Discussion: In order to most easily visualize relative performance, we place the security being analyzed as the numerator and the benchmark or base security as the denominator. This way, a rising line is consistent with outperformance of the security we are attempting to evaluate, avoiding the need to mentally invert a falling line if it was the denominator.

4. True or false: A rising relative strength (RS) line indicates that the stock being analyzed is increasing in value.

   Answer: False.

   Discussion: The RS line provides the analyst with information about relative performance only. A rising line can result when the security being analyzed is rising more quickly than the base security or if it is falling more slowly than the base security. When the RS line is declining, it implies the security being analyzed is falling more quickly than the base security or rising more slowly.

5. A(n) _____ provides the investor with general allocation guidelines while the markets themselves will help dictate how assets are ultimately diversified.

   Answer: A—Allocation range.

   Discussion: Individuals can establish ranges for the asset classes in which they feel comfortable investing, with these ranges reflecting the individual's constraints and preferences. The actual allocation ultimately chosen reflects the current market conditions, with stronger markets having allocations near the top of their range and weaker markets having allocations near the bottom of their range.

6. One approach to determining share size for a trade is using a maximum trade allocation value and dividing it by the _____, providing there is a rational maximum risk point for the trade.

   Answer: B—Current security price.

   Discussion: A trader who has already determined a maximum trade value can simply divide that value by the current security price when evaluating a trade. The actual position size can then be reduced for round lot trading, if desired. Since the trader will not know the actual purchase price until he is preparing to place the trade, adjustments may be required to reduce the position size if a large move occurred in the security since the initial analysis.

7. A portfolio is generally deemed riskier if it holds _____ asset(s) compared to _____ assets(s) that are not perfectly positively correlated.

   Answer: C—1 / 3.

   Discussion: Combining securities that are not perfectly positively correlated (i.e., do not move together perfectly) is the way to diversify holdings so that any declines in one security can be partially offset by less severe declines or advances in another security. The portfolio that holds just one security does not realize such protection. Although the opposite is true, that a single security portfolio could potentially realize better gains, this approach is not consistent with good risk management practices.

8. True or false: When traders diversify their strategies, they minimize their need to be right.

   Answer: True.

   Discussion: No trader can determine the future direction of a stock every trade. The goal in trading is to evaluate a security and establish a position when different indicators are pointing to a certain direction in order to improve the probability for profits. However, even the best analysis can prove to be incorrect when news hits the market or other factors impact price. By using different strategies (i.e., some more bullish, others capturing a volatility move) the trader does not need to rely on each analysis, which points in the same direction—being right.

MEDIA ASSIGNMENT

Risk management covers a number of different topics including the use of stop-losses, exit strategies, asset allocation, and diversification. In this media assignment, traders are encouraged to consider the impact of diversification and asset allocation using two different portfolios. The first includes $30,000 worth of QQQQ shares. In the other scenario, the investor purchases $10,000 of QQQQ shares, $10,000 of the iShares Long-Term Bond Fund (TLT), and $10,000 of the streetTracks Gold Fund (GLD). The idea is to get a feel about how various securities can perform differently over time.

For example, let's assume that these two portfolios were created on December 30, 2004, and see what happens during the year 2005. On the last day of trading in 2004, the QQQQ was trading for $40.00 a share, the TLT was at $88.50, and the GLD was near $43.86. Consequently, the two portfolios would look something like this at the time of purchase:

Portfolio 1

750 QQQQ Shares × $40.00
= $30,000

Portfolio 2

250 QQQQ shares × $40.00 = $10,000
113 TLT shares × $88.50 = $10,000
228 GLD shares × $43.86 = $10,000

$30,000

During the year 2005, the QQQQ rose from $40.00 a share to $40.41. Meanwhile, the TLT rose to $91.90 a share and the GLD rallied up to $51.58. So at the end of the year, the two portfolios would look like this:

Portfolio 1

750 QQQQ Shares × $40.41
= $30,308

Portfolio 2

250 QQQQ shares × $40.41 = $10,102.50
113 TLT shares × $91.90 = $10,384.70
228 GLD shares × $51.58 = $11,760.24

$32,247.44

In this example, the diversified portfolio easily beat the QQQQ portfolio. While the Qs rose only 1 percent, the mixed portfolio, thanks in big part to the rally in gold, rose 7.5 percent. Moreover, the diversified portfolio performed better with less volatility. The mean or average value of the QQQQ portfolio was $28,763 throughout the year. The low and high were $26,025 and $31,582, respectively, and the standard deviation was $1,291.50. Meanwhile, the diversified portfolio had a mean value of $30,087, a low and high of $28,645 and $32,550, and a standard deviation of $945. Therefore, the diversified portfolio not only beat the performance of the QQQQ portfolio, but also did so with less volatility.

VOCABULARY DEFINITIONS

Asset class: The broad categories of assets include stocks, bonds, commodities, real estate, and cash, and are referred to as asset classes.

Diversification: Investing or trading within different assets and/or groups.

Drawdown: The value of the reduction in equity for an account due to a losing trade.

Good till canceled (GTC): A brokerage order type that stands as an open order in the market until the trader or the brokerage firm cancels it—usually within 30 to 60 days. This type of order is generally used to place limit and stop orders.

Money management: On a broad scale, this term is used to describe how personal finances are handled through the planning process and allocation of funds, including trading funds.

Money market: A liquid, interest-bearing means of holding cash. Money market portfolio managers invest in very short-term, low credit risk instruments (i.e., T-Bills) in order to provide interest to those holding them.

Overlay chart: A type of chart that allows graphs of multiple securities to appear on a single chart. Generally two charts together are used by technicians, each using the right or left vertical axis for price data. As an option, the vertical axis may reflect relative price changes in the form of percentages instead.

Relative strength line: A ratio constructed on a chart used to compare relative movement between two securities. A rising line indicates that the security being evaluated (numerator) is outperforming the base or benchmark security (denominator).

Risk management: In the process of both protecting and growing assets, risk management refers to money allocations for specific accounts (investment versus trading), markets, and positions, and identifies maximum loss amounts. In addition to a plan that sets these figures, risk management includes the execution of the plan as well.

Risk tolerance: Individuals are limited by constraints and directed by preferences when making investment decisions. Preferences include risk tolerance, which is the amount of loss an individual is willing to accept given each unit of reward based on their unique marginal utility curves. Risk tolerance can change over time.

Stop-loss: The security value where the maximum loss allowed occurs is referred to as the stop-loss value. Stop-loss may also refer to the actual maximum loss allowed as well.

CHAPTER 15

Important Index Facts and Strategies

SUMMARY

Any trader seeking to truly understand index movements needs to determine the index components and construction methods, both of which are readily available to investors. There are three primary ways to construct an index: cap-weighted, equal-dollar-weighted, and price-weighted. In some instances larger-cap names will dominate index changes while in others the impact will be smaller. Once traders complete this first step, they are better able to select tracking products to implement their strategies.

We also take one more look at strategies toward the end of the chapter. Three index-based techniques are discussed that include index component changes, temporary changes between index pair movements, or boosting performance relative to an index. All of these techniques can be implemented with option strategies to create limited risk positions.

QUESTIONS AND EXERCISES

1. _____ is not an index construction method.
   A. Capitalization-weighted.
   B. Equal-dollar-weighted.
   C. Allocation-weighted.
   D. Price-weighted.

2. The S&P 500 is constructed using a(n) _____ method. As a result, the top 20 percent of the index accounts for 67 percent of its movement in 2005.

    A. Capitalization-weighted.

    B. Equal-dollar-weighted.

    C. Allocation-weighted.

    D. Price-weighted.

3. A benchmark index that measures the performance of a theoretical portfolio constructed of NASDAQ 100 companies and covered calls on the NDX is the _____.

    A. NASDAQ Buy Back Index (BUY).

    B. NASDAQ Composite Index (IXIC).

    C. NASDAQ 100 Options Trust (NOT).

    D. NASDAQ Buy Write Index (BXN).

4. True or false: Index components and structure generally remain fixed over long periods of time and require SEC approval for changes.

5. An index strategy using options that is similar to an options long strangle position is a(n) _____; this strategy seeks to benefit from temporary divergent movements in the securities.

    A. Pairs straddle.

    B. Natural straddle.

    C. Pairs spread.

    D. Inter-index spread.

6. When a company is added to an index, it generally moves _____, which is referred to as the _____ effect.

    A. Upward / out of circulation.

    B. Upward / index.

    C. Downward / out of circulation.

    D. Downward / index.

7. Maintaining a portfolio of securities designed to track a benchmark and adding a small position in which the manager has a bullish outlook will outperform the benchmark if the manager's assessment is correct. This strategy is known as a _____.

A. Nice year-end bonus.

B. Portfolio tilt.

C. Portfolio enhancement.

D. Bullish tilt.

8. True or false: Index construction information is considered highly proprietary and difficult to obtain.

MEDIA ASSIGNMENT

Chapter 15 includes a discussion about the construction or methodology used to create an index. Not all indexes are constructed the same way. Understanding the method used to compute the index can help traders make better sense of the index's daily moves. In other words, we sometimes want to dig inside the index to see what is really going on.

For this media assignment, we want to find the components and the product specifications for a specific index. The information can be found on the web site of the exchange where the options trade: the Chicago Board Options Exchange (www.cboe.com), the International Securities Exchange (www.iseoptions.com), the American Stock Exchange (www.amex.com), or the Philadelphia Stock Exchange (www.phlx.com).

In this example, the subject of study is the PHLX Semiconductor Index ($SOX). As the name of the index suggests, these options trade on the Philadelphia Stock Exchange (PHLX), so the first step is to type www.phlx.com into the web browser.

Once on the PHLX home page, identify and click on the "Products" tab. In the products area of the site, click on "Sector Index Options," and a table including a list of PHLX sector indexes will appears. Scroll down to the SOX index and click the link. From there, the reader will find complete contract specifications, including a description of the index, the settlement style, and a link to the component issues.

VOCABULARY LIST

Capitalization-weighted index	Inter-index spread
Divisor	Overweight
Equal-dollar-weighted index	Price-weighted index
Equal weight	Underweight

SOLUTIONS

1. _____ is not an index construction method.

   Answer: C—Allocation-weighted.

   Discussion: As far as we know, this is not an index construction method. The most popular construction methods include the capitalization-weighted method (S&P 500), the price-weighted index (Dow Jones Industrial Average), and an equal-dollar-weighted approach (CBOE Internet Index).

2. The S&P 500 is constructed using a(n) _____ method. As a result, the top 20 percent of the index accounts for 67 percent of its movement in 2005.

   Answer: A —Capitalization-weighted.

   Discussion: As mentioned in the previous answer, the S&P 500 is constructed using a cap-weighted method. Since the index itself holds many of the largest U.S. equities on any given day, it is easily seen that stock number 1 will have a much greater impact to index level changes than stock number 500. In fact, less than 20 percent of these top names represent more than half of the index movement.

3. A benchmark index that measures the performance of a theoretical portfolio constructed of NASDAQ 100 companies and covered calls on the NDX is the _____.

   Answer: D—NASDAQ Buy Write Index (BXN).

   Discussion: The NASDAQ Buy Write Index (BXN) measures the performance of a theoretical portfolio constructed of NASDAQ 100 companies and covered calls on the NDX, while the BXM index is constructed using a hypothetical portfolio of the S&P 500 with calls written against it, and the Dow Jones Buy Write Index ($BXD) measures the performance of a theoretical portfolio that sells DJX call options against a portfolio of Dow stocks.

4. True or false: Index components and structure generally remain fixed over long periods of time and require SEC approval for changes.

Answer: False.

Discussion: We threw the SEC bit in there to be sure readers understand that index components and construction can and do change periodically. In addition to companies being deleted from or added to an index, there are times when even certain construction methods can change. Consider the VIX discussed in Chapter 12.

5. An index strategy using options that is similar to an options long strangle position is a(n) _____; this strategy seeks to benefit from temporary divergent movements in the securities.

Answer: D—Inter-index spread.

Discussion: An inter-index spread is a strategy that uses pairs of two well-correlated indexes that have temporarily diverged from that correlation. The strategist is betting that one market will outperform another on a relative basis as they return to their longer-term, original relationship. When using options to benefit from the temporary disparity, a long call and long put with different strike prices are used, similar to a strangle. Although the underlying security is different for the put and the call, the strategist is seeking a move back to normal, which occurs when one moves more strongly than what is typical—this is how the disparity arose in the first place.

6. When a company is added to an index, it generally moves _____, which is referred to as the _____ effect.

Answer: B—Upward / index.

Discussion: As institutional funds that track the benchmark purchase the security being added to the index, demand moves price upward. This is defined as the index effect. There are trading strategies that seek to benefit from this effect.

7. Maintaining a portfolio of securities designed to track a benchmark and adding a small position in which the manager has a bullish outlook will outperform the benchmark if the manager's assessment is correct. This strategy is known as a _____.

Answer: B—Portfolio tilt.

Discussion: Strategists seeking to beat the S&P 500 will hold securities that track the index, and at the same time increase their exposure to the securities that they believe will outperform the index, so that the whole portfolio beats the benchmark. Similarly, in terms of portfolio management, an investor may increase shares of a specific security or sector to increase its percent allocation in the portfolio due to a bullish outlook for that security or sector. This can be accomplished with ETFs, stock, or call options on either. An alternative approach is to underweight weaker performers by adding put positions. This, too, is known as a portfolio tilt.

8. True or false: Index construction information is considered highly proprietary and difficult to obtain.

   Answer: False.

   Discussion: Although component selection can occur behind closed doors, the method for calculating index levels is generally an open one. The best place to access information on a particular index is by going to the source, such as Standard & Poor's, Dow Jones, Russell, and the like.

MEDIA ASSIGNMENT

When looking at the product information for a specific index, traders want to ask themselves several questions. First, how do these options settle? For example, looking at the product specification for the PHLX Semiconductor Index ($SOX), which is the media assignment for this chapter, reveals that the options on the SOX settle American style. What does this mean? It means that these options can be exercised or assigned at any time prior to expiration.

So the semiconductor index is one of the few cash indexes that settle American style. Most indexes settle European style, which means that exercise and assignment can only occur at expiration. While most indexes have the European-style exercise feature, stocks and exchange-traded funds settle American style.

Next, we want to consider the number of components and the methodology used to compute the index. At the time of this writing, the PHLX Semiconductor Index has 19 different chip stocks.

In addition, it uses the price-weighted methodology. Therefore, the higher-priced stocks will have a greater influence on the performance of the index when compared to lower-priced stocks. Table 15.1 shows the 19 components of the index and their respective weightings as of December 2005. At that time, Marvel Technology (MRVL) had the highest price and the greatest weighting. The lowest-priced stock, Infineon Technologies (IFX), had the smallest weighting.

The product specification information on the exchange's web site will include other facts such as the last day to trade the options (on Thursday before expiration for the SOX), the expiration cycle, and how the settlement value is calculated. Index traders will want to know a lot of this information before trading the contract.

In sum, it is important to know where to find the index facts. The information is on the web site where the options are listed for trading—the Chicago Board Options Exchange (www.cboe.com), the International Securities Exchange (www.iseoptions.com), the American Stock Exchange (www.amex.com), or the Philadelphia Stock Exchange (www.phlx.com).

TABLE 15.1 SOX Components

SOX Component	Symbol	Price	Weighting
Altera Corp.	ALTR	19.10	3.61%
Applied Materials, Inc.	AMAT	18.33	3.47%
Advanced Micro Devices	AMD	32.40	6.12%
Broadcom Corporation	BRCM	48.58	9.18%
Freescale Semiconductor, Inc.	FSLB	25.35	4.79%
Infineon Technologies AG	IFX	9.45	1.79%
Intel Corp.	INTC	25.57	4.83%
KLA-Tencor Corp.	KLAC	50.69	9.58%
Linear Technology Corp.	LLTC	36.77	6.95%
Marvel Technology Group	MRVL	58.17	11.00%
Micron Technology, Inc.	MU	13.51	2.55%
Maxim Integrated Products, Inc.	MXIM	37.15	7.02%
National Semiconductor Corp.	NSM	26.95	5.09%
Novellus Systems, Inc.	NVLS	24.47	4.63%
STMicroelectronics NV	STM	18.60	3.52%
Teradyne, Inc.	TER	14.78	2.79%
Taiwan Semiconductor Manufacturing	TSM	10.10	1.91%
Texas Instruments, Inc.	TXN	33.24	6.28%
Xilinx, Inc.	XLNX	25.77	4.87%

VOCABULARY DEFINITIONS

Capitalization-weighted index: When computing a cap-weighted index, the sums of the market caps (shares traded times market price) are added together and the sum is divided by its divisor.

Divisor: A numeric value that incorporates the total number of index components and also makes an adjustment for various corporate activities in these underlying securities so that changes in the index reflect only price changes due to supply and demand factors.

Equal-dollar-weighted index: One method that is growing in popularity is the equal-dollar method. In this case, the builders of the index assume that the same dollar amount is invested in each stock within the index.

Equal weight: A balanced portfolio that allocates its dollars to mirror the allocations of the benchmark it is tracking. It does not overweight or underweight any securities in the portfolio and seeks only to match the benchmark's performance.

Inter-index spread: An inter-index spread is a strategy that uses pairs of two well-correlated indexes that have temporarily diverged from that correlation. The strategist is betting that one market will outperform another on a relative basis as they return to their longer-term, original relationship.

Overweight: In terms of portfolio management, adding shares of a specific security or sector to increase its percent allocation in the portfolio due to a bullish outlook for that security or sector. In particular, if a manager seeks to beat the S&P 500, he will hold securities that track the index and add securities he believes will outperform the index so that the whole portfolio beats the benchmark.

Price-weighted index: A price-weighted index is simply an average of the stock prices within the index. It was the method used to compute the first average: Simply add up the stock prices and divide by the number of companies (or components) within the index.

Underweight: In terms of portfolio management, reducing shares of a specific security or sector to decrease its percent allocation in the portfolio due to a bearish outlook for that security or sector. In particular, if a manager seeks to beat the S&P 500, he will hold securities that track the index and reduce his exposure to securities he believes will underperform the index so that the whole portfolio beats the benchmark.

CHAPTER 16

Getting Started

SUMMARY

This final chapter provides newer traders with basic broker and account information to help navigate these critical areas. Details on paper trading are also provided so that individuals have an opportunity to practice any strategy that is new to them—regardless of whether they have experience with other strategies. The focus for this chapter is options trading since there are some unique broker and paper trading considerations for options. The information provided is easily extended to trading stocks and exchange-traded funds (ETFs).

We wrap up the text with information about order types as part of trade management. Individuals need to know in advance whether execution or price is a priority for the trade—once that is determined there are a few alternatives available to them. Since risk management is a priority for all trades, when you must exit a position, simply get out—do not attempt to use complicated orders that may or may not be executed.

QUESTIONS AND EXERCISES

1. Cost is _____ consideration when selecting a discount broker.
   A. The only.
   B. One.
   C. Not a.
   D. None of the above.

2. Adding options trading to your account requires _____.
   A. Checking a box on your brokerage application.
   B. SEC approval.
   C. Specific approval from the broker.
   D. Five years stock trading experience.

3. Paper trading can be documented by hand or via the Internet using a(n) _____.
   A. Portfolio tracker.
   B. Active brokerage account.
   C. Futures trading account.
   D. All of the above.

4. True or false: Retirement accounts are ideal places to short stock.

5. The _____ is the type of order to use when you must exit a trade—it guarantees execution but not price.
   A. Limit order.
   B. Fill or kill.
   C. Market order.
   D. Good till canceled.

6. The _____ is the type of order to use when you wish to exit a trade at a specific price, recognizing that the order may not be filled.
   A. Limit order.
   B. Fill or kill.
   C. Market order.
   D. Good till canceled.

7. An options trader may elect to _____ a position when it has _____ time premium remaining.
   A. Sell / little.
   B. Exercise / no.
   C. Exercise / valuable.
   D. Sell / no.

8. True or false: A stop order triggers a market order while a stop limit order triggers a limit order.

MEDIA ASSIGNMENT

This media assignment requires access to the Internet. The reader/strategist will create a paper trade on the Optionetics Portfolio Tracker or a similar tracker using the trade constructed in the media assignment for Chapter 6. In the event a period of time has passed since completing the assignment from Chapter 6, and the option expiration dates are no longer available, construct a similar paper trade for this assignment. Once the paper trade is established, monitor the position as you would with a real trade. Identify risk management rules, including exit strategies.

VOCABULARY LIST

Buy on close (also market on close)

Buy on open (also market on open)

Cancel former order (also one cancels other)

Day order

Exercise

Margin

Market order

Paper trading

Portfolio tracker

Retirement account

Sell on close (also market on close)

Sell on open (also market on open)

Stop limit order

Stop order

Trading level

SOLUTIONS

1. Cost is _____ consideration when selecting a discount broker.

   Answer: B—One.

   Discussion: Cost due to commissions and account fees is important when selecting a broker, but not at the expense of execution and ease of use. First and foremost is the ability to make option trades and make them seamlessly and quickly.

2. Adding options trading to your account requires _____.

   Answer: C—Specific approval from the broker.

   Discussion: Not all accounts are eligible for options trading and, once approved, not all traders have access to all options strategies. Individuals who seek to trade options must submit an option approval form to their broker that identifies trading experience and discloses a variety of financial information. The broker must determine the approval level appropriate for the account based on account type, trader experience, and financial status.

3. Paper trading can be documented by hand or via the Internet using a(n) _____.

   Answer: A—Portfolio tracker.

   Discussion: Although the emotions experienced are not completely replicated when you paper trade, it remains a very rational approach for new traders to initiate trading and for experienced traders to experiment with new strategies. A portfolio tracker allows a trader to enter mock trades, track them, and see how they fare over time using paper money.

4. True or false: Retirement accounts are ideal places to short stock.

   Answer: False.

   Discussion: No way! First, short selling requires margin trading, which is not an option for retirement accounts. Keep in mind that short selling stock is a limited-reward, unlimited-risk strategy and not one that is advocated for short-term trading, let along long-term investments.

5. The _____ is the type of order to use when you must exit a trade—it guarantees execution but not price.

   Answer: C—Market order.

   Discussion: When a trader feels he must exit a trade, he should simply exit it—not use a more complicated approach that guarantees price but not execution. A market order is the type of trade that guarantees execution. When using such an order, it is best to enter the order when the market is open so the trader can see the current market for the position; however, this is not more important than having the order in place. Don't wait until you can be available during market hours to enter the order. The downside with such an order is that price is not guaranteed—a trade can be executed at a price substantially different from the current market if entered when the markets are closed.

6. The _____ is the type of order to use when you wish to exit a trade at a specific price, recognizing that the order may not be filled.

   Answer: A—Limit order.

   Discussion: A limit order guarantees price but not execution. Assuming a trader wants to sell a security at a price higher than the current market, he or she can enter a limit order above the market price. The only way the trade will be executed is if the market reaches that level. The order can be entered as a good till canceled (GTC) order so that it remains in the market for a certain period of time.

7. An options trader may elect to _____ a position when it has _____ time premium remaining.

   Answer: B—Exercise / no.

   Discussion: When deciding whether to sell a long option or exercise when the trader wishes to own the underlying (call) or sell the underlying (put), the trader needs to determine if there is any time value remaining in the contract. If so, the option should be sold to avoid forfeiting this component of the option's value, while simultaneously executing the appropriate stock transaction in the market. Exercise will generally occur when there is no time value in the option, which typically occurs when the option is deep in-the-money. One advantage to exercising the option is that there is a fixed strike price—no market slippage will occur.

8. True or false: A stop order triggers a market order while a stop limit order triggers a limit order.

Answer: True.

Discussion: Although we did not formally discuss a stop limit order, we hope the reader was able to distinguish these order types. Both stop orders and stop limit orders generate the corresponding order type when a trigger is reached—it is as if the trader was monitoring the markets and entering a market or limit order once the trigger conditions were in place.

MEDIA ASSIGNMENT

This media assignment makes use of a portfolio tracker. In the example provided we use the Optionetics.com tracker, which requires free registration to access and maintain the portfolio. Recall from Chapter 6 the calendar spread in Table 16.1.

Once online we proceed to www.optionetics.com and click on the sixth tab, "My Portfolio." The user can register, log in, or access the help page, which appears in Figure 16.1.

Both registration and portfolio creation are extremely user friendly and straightforward. Option symbols must be preceded by the letter O with a colon ("O:"). The portfolio was named *Put Calendar* and the ETF IBB was added to the portfolio so its price could be easily tracked with the option prices. Since no position was actually established for IBB, the value of 0 was entered for number of shares purchased; however, the purchase date of December 22, 2005, and price of $78.18 were added.

Figure 16.2 is a view of the put calendar portfolio tracker that was completed in less than five minutes.

TABLE 16.1 Call Calendar Analysis

Call Calendar Spread	Symbol	Recent Price	Long/Short	Cost of Spread
iShares Biotech	IBB	78.18		
Jan 80 Call	IBBAP	0.85	Ask (short)	−0.85
Mar 80 Call	IBBCP	2.70	Bid (long)	+2.70
				+1.85

FIGURE 16.1 Portfolio Tracker Help Page (*Source:* www.Optionetics.com)

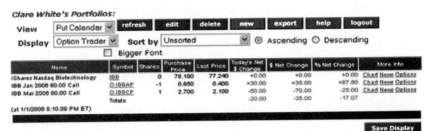

FIGURE 16.2 Put Calendar Portfolio Tracker (*Source:* www.Optionetics.com)

VOCABULARY DEFINITIONS

Buy on close (also market on close): This type of order provides the trader with an execution near the closing price for a security.

Buy on open (also market on open): This type of order provides the trader with an execution near the opening price for a security.

Cancel former order (also one cancels other): When a trader wishes to change an existing order, it is best to enter a change order (a.k.a. cancel former order), rather than closing the existing order, waiting to receive confirmation the order has been canceled, and then creating a new one. By changing an existing order, the new order is sent to the market and the original order canceled. However, if it is too late to cancel the original order because it has already been executed, the revised order will not be sent. One order cancels the other.

Day order: An order that remains open for the entire trading session in which it is opened. In the event the market is closed when the order is placed, it will stand throughout the next trading day.

Exercise: To implement the right of the holder of an option to buy (in the case of a call) or sell (in the case of a put) the underlying security. When you exercise an option, you carry out the terms of an option contract.

Margin: Amounts deposited into an account when an investor borrows money from a broker for the purpose of establishing a securities position. The margin required for specific positions varies, but is a minimum of 50 percent for long stock purchases. The margin requirement for a short position is minimally 150 percent—100 percent is deposited in the account from the sale of the security and at least another 50 percent is deposited by the account holder. Short option positions have margin calculations that are based partly on the margin requirements of the underlying security and partly on the protection provided by a second option on the underlying, as appropriate.

Market order: An order that guarantees execution, but not price. When a market order is placed, the trader's order should be filled close to the current market seen; however, the actual execution is based on the speed of the markets and the trader's order priority.

Paper trading: A method of simulating a trade in an investment account, which can be completed manually or via a web tool. Paper trading gives a trader the opportunity to practice a new strategy without placing real money on the line. It allows both new and experienced traders to gain insight on how a position will move relative to changes in market conditions.

Portfolio tracker: A web-based service that allows traders to enter stock and option trades and track them in one area. Portfolio trackers are great tools for placing option paper trades since the trader can readily review a multi-leg option position along with the underlying security and observe the movements of all the securities as well as the position gain or loss.

Retirement account: A brokerage account that is held by a firm on your behalf. This type of account has different tax treatment; assets may be deposited pre- or post-tax and gains may be tax-deferred or tax-free. Contact your broker or accountant for additional information.

Sell on close (also market on close): The sell side of *buy on close.*

Sell on open (also market on open): The sell side of *buy on open.*

Stop limit order: An order that triggers a limit order when the stop level is reached. When selling a security, the stop is placed below the current market price and the limit is at a level designated by the trader.

Stop order: An order that triggers a market order when the stop level is reached. When selling a security, the stop is placed below the current market price. It is similar to monitoring the price of the security and entering a market order once a certain price is reached.

Trading level: The option strategy approval for the account, as dictated by the brokerage firm's compliance group, is referred to as the trading level. Factors impacting the option trading level include the account type, the experience of all account holders, and the financial standing of all account holders.

Frequently Asked Questions

INDEX TRADING

Q. What is an index?

An index is a benchmark used to track a basket or group of stocks. For example, the S&P 500 Index ($SPX) is an index based on the share prices of 500 of the largest companies that have stocks listed on the U.S. exchanges. This index is considered a benchmark for the performance of the U.S. stock market. The Dow Jones Industrial Average ($INDU) and the NASDAQ Composite ($COMPQ) are also market indexes.

Q. Are indexes new?

Indexes are not new. In fact, Charles Dow created the first official index in 1884. At that time, it was known as the Dow Jones Railroad Average. The name has since changed to the Dow Jones Transportation Average. The second average, published in 1896, is today's Dow Jones Industrial Average.

Q. What are other examples of indexes?

A large number of indexes exist today—too many for investors to track them all. In addition to market averages such as the Dow and the S&P 500

Index, a variety of sector indexes also exists. Examples include the PHLX Semiconductor Index ($SOX), the AMEX Biotechnology Index ($BTK), and the CBOE Internet Index ($INX). Some indexes track specific segments of the market, such as the Russell 2000 Small Cap Index ($RUT), the S&P MidCap Index ($MID), and the Dogs of the Dow Index ($MUT). Table A.1 lists some of the more widely followed indexes.

Q. How are indexes computed?

The first index was simply an average of the closing prices of a dozen railroad stocks. The methodology is different today. Due to stock splits and dividends, the calculation of an index is a bit more complicated. With most indexes, the stock prices or the market values of the companies are added together and the index value is derived using a divisor. Using a divisor rather than a simple average or mean ensures that an index will not fall in value when stocks split or pay dividends.

Q. How do I invest in an index? Can I buy shares?

It is not possible to buy into or invest directly into an index. They are benchmarks and not investments. However, it is possible to buy into exchange-traded funds (ETF) that mimic specific indexes. These so-called

TABLE A.1 Popular Indexes

DJ Utility Average	DUX	NASDAQ 100 Index	NDX
PHLX Bank Index	BKX	NYSE Composite Index	NYA
AMEX Biotech Index	BTK	S&P 100 Index	OEX
AMEX Consumer Product Index	CMR	PHLX Oil Service Index	OSX
MS Commodity Related Index	CRX	Russell 2000 Small Cap Index	RUT
MS Cyclical Index	CYC	S&P Growth Index	SGX
AMEX Defense Index	DFX	PHLX Semiconductor Index	SOX
DJ Industrial Average	DJX	S&P 500 Index	SPX
AMEX Pharmaceutical Index	DRG	PHLX Steel Index	STQ
GSTI Computer Hardware Index	GHA	S&P Value Index	SVX
GSTI Computer Software Index	GSO	CBOE Ten Year Rate Index	TNX
PHLX Homebuilders Index	HGX	DJ Transports	DTX
CBOE Internet Index	INX	AMEX Airline Index	XAL
PHLX Mortgage Finance Index	MFX	PHLX Gold Mining Index	XAU
S&P MidCap Index	MID	AMEX Broker/Dealer Index	XBD
CBOE Dogs of the Dow Index	MUT	AMEX Oil Index	XOI

tracking stocks hold the same stocks as the index. For example, the most actively traded ETF today is the NASDAQ 100 Index Trust (QQQQ). It holds the same 100 stocks as the NASDAQ 100 Index ($NDX), which includes the top 100 nonfinancial stocks that trade on the NASDAQ Stock Market. The QQQQ is designed to equal 1/40 of the NASDAQ 100 Index. Meanwhile, the Dow Jones diamonds (DIA) is an ETF that holds the same 30 stocks as the Dow Jones Industrial Average, and the S&P 500 Depositary Receipts (SPY) holds the S&P 500 stocks.

Q. Can I sell short an index?

No. Short selling is a bearish bet that involves borrowing shares from a broker and selling them in the market. Shares of indexes do not trade and it is therefore not possible to sell them short. However, it is possible to sell short exchange-traded funds like the QQQQ, SPY, or DIA.

Q. Are options listed on indexes?

Options are available on many, but not all, indexes. The first index option was listed on the S&P 100 Index ($OEX) in 1983, 10 years after the start of stock option trading. Ten years later, the Chicago Board Options Exchange (CBOE) launched the CBOE Volatility Index ($VIX), which tracks the implied volatility (IV) of S&P index options.

Q. How do index options settle?

Index options settle for cash, and therefore exercise and assignment involve the transfer of cash, not shares. The amount is equal to the difference between the strike price of the option and the settlement value of the index.

Q. What is a European-style index?

Most index options settle European-style, which means that exercise or assignment can only take place at expiration. By contrast, options on stocks and exchange-traded funds settle American-style, whereby exercise and assignment can occur at any time prior to expiration.

Q. Which indexes settle American-style?

While there are not many, a few cash indexes do settle American-style. Examples include the S&P 100 Index ($OEX), the PHLX Semiconductor Index ($SOX), and the AMEX Oil Index ($XOI).

Q. What kinds of strategies work well with indexes?

Indexes can be used to speculate or to hedge. For example, put options on
the S&P 500 Index can be used to hedge a portfolio of stocks if the investor is concerned about a market decline or crash. Additionally, strategists can establish bullish or bearish trades based on the outlook for an
index. For example, a trader who expects chip stocks to rally during the
fourth quarter can establish a bull call spread on the PHLX Semiconductor
Index. In fact, any strategy that can be applied using stock options and
does not require shares can be used on indexes.

Q. Why should I trade indexes rather than stocks?

There is no specific reason to trade indexes rather than stocks. An index
will generally be less volatile than a stock because it consists of many
stocks and has more diversification. In other words, an index will not
make the large one-day moves that are sometimes possible with stocks. In
addition, the analysis of the index market is different than with stocks.
For example, while a stock trader might focus on an upcoming earnings
report, a new product launch, or a management shake-up, index traders
often pay greater attention to macroeconomic trends such as changes in
interest rates, oil prices, or other economic news.

Q. Is it possible to trade indexes using charts?

Yes, the same indicators and technical analysis tools that are used on
stocks can be applied to indexes.

**Q. Where can I find a complete list of indexes and each index's
components?**

The stock and options exchanges that trade index options have product
specification information on their web sites. The list includes the Chicago
Board Options Exchange (CBOE), the American Stock Exchange
(AMEX), the Philadelphia Stock Exchange (PHLX) and the International
Securities Exchange (ISE).

**Q. Finally, are index traders, on average, better looking and more
intelligent than stock option traders?**

Yes, definitely!

EXCHANGE-TRADED FUNDS

Q. What does ETF stand for and what does it mean?

ETF is short for exchange-traded fund. It is a type of pooled investment vehicle similar to a mutual fund. However, unlike a mutual fund, which sells shares directly to investors, ETFs trade on the stock exchanges including the American Stock Exchange (AMEX), the NASDAQ Stock Market, and the New York Stock Exchange (NYSE).

Q. What are some examples of exchange-traded funds?

The most actively traded ETFs today include the NASDAQ 100 Index Trust (QQQQ), the Dow Jones Diamonds (DIA), and the S&P 500 Depositary Receipts (SPY).

Q. How do I invest in exchange-traded funds? Are options available?

Exchange-traded funds are bought and sold through a broker, like shares of stock. Many, but not all, ETFs have listed options. In fact, the options on the QQQQ are the most actively traded contract today. Options on ETFs are bought and sold through a broker like stock options.

Q. Do ETF options settle like index options or like stock options?

Options on exchange-traded funds settle like stock options. That is, they settle American-style, so exercise or assignment can occur at any time prior to expiration. By contrast, index options settle European-style, and exercise or assignment can only take place at expiration. In addition, index options settle for cash. However, settlement of ETF and stock options involves the physical delivery of shares.

Q. Are futures available on exchange-traded funds?

Yes. In June 2005, the Chicago Mercantile Exchange (CME) started listing options on the NASDAQ 100 Index Trust (QQQQ), the S&P 500 Depositary Receipts (SPY), and the Russell 2000 Small Cap Fund (IWM).

Q. Can investors sell short exchange-traded funds?

Short selling is a strategy that requires borrowing shares, selling them, and buying them back later. It is a bearish strategy because it makes profits from a move south in the security. Most ETFs can be sold short. However, this is sometimes difficult to do with less actively traded funds. You might check with your broker before placing an order to sell short an ETF.

Q. If ETFs are pooled investments, what types of securities do they hold?

Most exchange-traded funds hold a basket of stocks. Some are created around specific indexes. For example, the Dow Jones diamonds holds the same 30 stocks as the Dow Jones Industrial Average ($INDU), and the S&P Depositary Receipts holds the same stocks as the S&P 500 Index ($SPX). Other ETFs are created around specific industry groups. Examples include the NASDAQ Biotechnology Index (IBB), the Semiconductor HOLDRs (SMH), and the PowerShares Dynamic Biotech & Genome Portfolio (PBE).

Q. Do ETFs hold assets other than stocks?

Yes, some of these funds will hold real estate, commodities, and sometimes bonds. For example, the iShares Long-Term Bond Fund (TLT) holds a basket of long-term government bonds. The streetTracks Gold Fund (GLD) holds gold. An oil ETF is in the works.

Q. How many exchange-traded funds exist today?

Since the launch of the S&P Depositary Receipts (SPY), or "spiders," in the early 1990s, exchange-traded funds have grown significantly in number. Today there are approximately 350 ETFs worldwide and almost 200 in the United States.

Q. Where can I find a complete list of exchange-traded funds?

The stock and options exchanges that trade ETF shares, futures, and options have product specification information on their web sites. The list includes the NYSE, the Chicago Board Options Exchange, the NASDAQ

Stock Market, the AMEX, the Chicago Mercantile Exchange, and the International Securities Exchange.

Q. Is it possible that the recent enthusiasm for exchange-traded funds is simply a passing phase or a fad?

The ETF industry is here to stay. During the past 10 years, the assets held in ETFs have skyrocketed from $1 billion to about $296 billion at the end of 2005. Average daily turnover worldwide exceeds $12 billion. In short, the number of ETFs and the assets held continues to grow, and there is every reason to believe the growth in the industry is much more than simply a short-term fad.

FREE Trading Package

(A $100 VALUE)

FROM GEORGE A. FONTANILLS AND TOM GENTILE

Request your FREE Trading Package and learn more about high-profit, low-risk, low-stress trading strategies *that really work*!

The Trading Package is full of practical tips and useful information to guide you down the path toward successful trading. The trading fundamentals presented are based on the same proven techniques taught by Optionetics (www.optionetics.com), which was founded by George Fontanills in 1993 to show individual investors how to profit in all market conditions. Since that time, Optionetics has become a leading provider of investment education services, portfolio management techniques, market analysis, and online trading tools to more than 250,000 people from more than 50 countries worldwide.

To receive your FREE Trading Package, simply complete and mail (or fax) the form below to:

Optionetics
P.O. Box 2409
Santa Rosa, CA 95404
Fax: 650-802-0900

You may also call 888-366-8264 (or 650-802-0700 outside of the United States), or e-mail customerservice@optionetics.com.

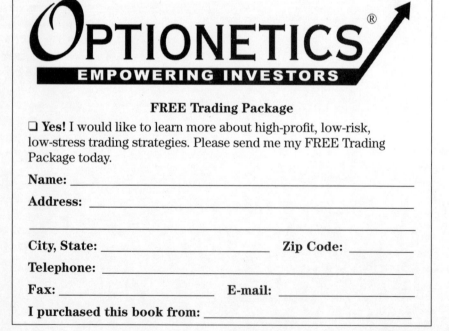

FREE Trading Package

❑ **Yes!** I would like to learn more about high-profit, low-risk, low-stress trading strategies. Please send me my FREE Trading Package today.

Name: _____

Address: _____

_____

City, State: _____   **Zip Code:** _____

Telephone: _____

Fax: _____   **E-mail:** _____

I purchased this book from: _____